Restroom

Contemporary design

Dedication
One, two, three, four, five
Once I caught a fish alive
Six, seven, eight, nine, ten
Then I let it go again.

This book is dedicated to *mon petit chou*, le pêcheur.

Published in 2008
by Laurence King Publishing Ltd
361–373 City Road
London EC1V 1LR
Tel +44 20 7841 6900
Fax +44 20 7841 6910
E-mail enquiries@laurenceking.co.uk
www.laurenceking.co.uk

A catalogue record for this book is available from the British Library.

ISBN 978 1 85669 518 3

Designed by John Round Design

Printed in China

Laurence King Publishing

Restroom

Contemporary design

Jennifer Hudson

Contents

Introduction

Going to the toilet, like sex, disease and death, is a taboo subject. Most people are reticent to talk about their bodily functions yet, based on the premise that we spend eight minutes per day on the toilet, in total we pass at least three years of our lives engaged in this activity. Many a euphemism exists for 'the smallest room in the house' in which we 'spend a penny', 'have a tinkle' or 'send a fax to Darmstadt'. We refer to the toilet, the bathroom, the restroom, the powder room, the can, the john, the privy, the bog, or use countless other expressions, to disguise the fact that we have to excuse ourselves and do what everyone else has to do.

The word toilet can be used to refer to the fixture itself or the room containing it, although the latter predominates in Britain and the Commonwealth, while in North America it refers solely to the product and not the room itself. Asking for the toilet in the United States would appear indecent, so instead people refer to the bathroom, the restroom or the washroom. Wherever you are, however, the toilet is noted as the great unifier of humanity because people of all social classes must use it: in Poland, there is the saying *gdzie nawet król chodzi pieçhota* ('where even the king walks by himself') and a similar expression was used in imperial Germany. Yet in Britain this was not always the case; the use of the word toilet carried class connotations. In 1954, the landed novelist Nancy Mitford, who wrote about aristocratic life in England and France, popularized the famous 'U', or upper-class, and non-'U' classification of linguistic usage and behaviour. Many of the non-'U' words derived from Victorian times when they were adopted by the lower classes competing to appear more refined. These included words with French derivation and such was the case with toilet, which came from *toilette*, the French word for getting ready, washing and dressing. The upper class then shunned the word as an *arriviste* affectation. The toilet, loo or bathroom (however you prefer to call it) is not only a part of our everyday life, but also of the history of human hygiene and, as such, the history of civilization.

Toilets in one form or another have existed since man started building cities and over the ages have reflected cultural mores and social prejudices. Archaeological remains in the palace of King Minos in Crete reveal indoor plumbing in 2,000 BC, while in the Orkney Islands 4,800-year-old toilets have been unearthed. Stone benches, with holes and watercourses beneath, have existed in Greece and Egypt; in the temples of the Incas and the ancient sites of the Indus Valley, in what is today Pakistan. Bathing and excreting remained a public activity for centuries. With the motto 'plumbing for the people', the Romans were famous for their public baths, as well as their communal latrines, which held up to 80 people. The small space between the users, no more than 50–60 centimetres (20–24 inches), meant these well-ventilated rooms were places of social interaction, where no expense was spared on elaborate marble seats and mosaics to make the daily activity congenial. Sanitation may have disintegrated along with the Roman Empire but there was still no social taboo associated with excretion. The Middle Ages literally stank: people defecated in public, over cess-pits

or in outhouses marked with a heart cut in the door. Chamber pots were emptied into the street encouraging vermin, and diseases and epidemics were rife. Only the monasteries with the communal *necessarium* which washed effluence away through designed watercourses escaped the worst of the Black Death, the pandemic which is estimated to have killed between a third and two thirds of Europe's population in the fourteenth century.

Change only came about in the eighteenth century when the supporters of the Age of Enlightenment (the European intellectual movement that advocated Reason as the primary basis of authority) demanded scientific progress in everyday life. Although the water closet had been developed in 1589 by John Harrington, it wasn't until Alexander Cummings invented the 'S' Trap in 1775 that all the components for the flushing toilet were in place.

With the advent of such a system, civilization found a means of disassociating an individual from his or her own excreta. The development of sewerage systems in major cities in Europe and the United States during the nineteenth century was an elaborate mechanism for the public processing of private waste which, as well as safeguarding against the frequent outbreaks of cholera at the time, was also seen as a symbol of social order. The Victorian era was one of contradictions. A plethora of social movements concerned with improving public morals co-existed with a class system that permitted harsh living conditions for many. A growing concern with sanitation existed not only to protect against disease but also to alleviate the repugnance that a rising middle-class felt towards their inferiors' smelliness and lack of cleanliness. Bourgeois Victorian morality, which extended far beyond the boundaries of England and her colonies, espoused sexual repression and a strong social ethic, and dictated that going to the toilet was something never to be mentioned in polite society. It was instead to be done behind closed doors, and the results rendered invisible, unscented and above all anonymous – disposed of as discreetly and hygienically as possible into the communal sewers. What had once been an activity as free of shame as brushing one's hair became invested with feelings of embarrassment and disgust, and the toilet was transformed into a public demonstration of refinement and superiority as well as a temple of privacy. Much of our psychological subjugation of 'the natural' can be traced back to this time, when talk of sex and bodily functions associated with sexualized body parts was disapproved of and discouraged.

If the restraint and disguise of natural functions was at first imposed consciously to differentiate the social and moral position of those imposing the rules over a class they felt to be their subordinate, the years following Queen Victoria's death resulted in a major shift of socio-economic and cultural conditions in Britain and throughout the world. As society gradually became less hierarchical and people more equal and reliant on one another, the social reference to shame or embarrassment receded to be replaced by more internal, subconscious and automatic feelings of disgust at our own bodily functions; an aversion compounded by the early conditioning of children to behave correctly in abstract terms of morality and hygiene.

1

2

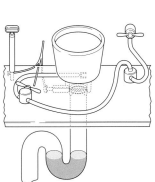

3

4

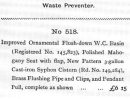

5

6

7

1 Public Roman latrine, Villa del Casale in Piazza Armerina, Sicily, fourth century AD. Communal toilets were usually situated near to commercial or social centres and could serve up to 80 people sitting 50–60 centimetres (20–24 inches) apart. Human waste was flushed by a constant flow of water running throughout the building. Heated and decorated with sumptuous mosaics and ornate fountains, the latrines were places to sit and read, or catch up on the latest intrigues.

2 Medieval stone outhouse, Pont Aven, Brittany, France. In the Middle Ages going to the toilet was still uninhibited but lacked the sociability it did for the ancient civilizations. People used chamber pots or visited primitive wooden structures protuding from the top floor of buildings; both were emptied directly into the streets. Alternatively stone privies were attached to castles and bridges; the wastes were disposed of in the moat or the flowing river below.

3 The first water toilet (named 'The Ajax') was invented in 1589 by the Englishman John Harrington for his godmother, Queen Elizabeth I. At the time the concept was ridiculed but would not have succeeded for lack of a systemized drainage system. The closet had a pan with an opening at the bottom, sealed with a leather-faced valve. A system of levers and weights poured in water, which opened the valve and flushed away the waste.

4 Louis XIV's 'Gentleman of the Royal Bed Chamber and wiper of the Royal Bum' (1700). The morning toilet and reception (the levée) of Louis XIV became a model for princes throughout Europe. The process could take up to an hour, and nobles were expected to attend him. Servants were assigned the job of cleaning the royal behind with wool or lace for added comfort. The toilet routines of the 'Sun King' also included taking meals and conducting meetings of state while on the commode with an audience present.

5 The first patented toilet was registered in 1775 by Alexander Cummings who devised the 'S' bend which for the first time allowed man to be separated from his own excreta.

6 Thomas Crapper might have lent his name to what we do on the toilet but he was not its inventor. Active in the period between 1861 and 1904, he registered nine patents and popularized the use of porcelain for the pan. Often decorated with patterns similar to those on expensive dinnerware, the toilet was elevated to a luxury item.

7 The Victorian sewers were the work of one of the nineteenth century's greatest engineers, Sir Joseph Bazalgette. The 132 kilometres (82 miles) of sewers were approved in 1858, during the 'Great Stink' when the stench from the Thames forced Parliament to rise. As well as safe-guarding against disease the sewers were also seen as symbols of a healthy social order.

At this time, Sigmund Freud referred to the anal stage of development, when the primary focus of the libido is on controlling bladder and bowel movements. Children have to learn to be in charge of their bodily needs which, if successfully achieved, will lead to a sense of accomplishment and independence; but if handled incorrectly will result in neurosis, and possibly special scatological practices and ceremonies carefully carried out in secret.

The essentially private nature of what goes on behind the closed doors of the bathroom, in conjunction with the powerful metaphor of the toilet as a container of our unclean urges means that this, often tiny, room is destined to be of primal importance both emotionally as well as biologically. Here we are stripped of all illusions and accoutrements of civilization and left to confront ourselves. The bathroom is the place where all our unsavoury activities can be dealt with hygienically in nice clean porcelain fixtures, containerized and sanitized in well-designed environments that will take our mind off what we are there to perform.

The taboo, however, also has a strange and perverse attraction and the best way to deal with that is humour. A process which begins unconsciously at school (usually the first time we are forced to share a restroom with others, when the use of forbidden words and jokes about body parts masks our, as yet, undefined embarrassment) becomes a conscious psychological distancing technique in adulthood. For thousands of years, this has given rise to the latrinalia which, evoking reactions of disgust and/or ribald delight, has adorned restroom walls from the Roman forum to today's bars and clubs. Present culture is rampant with bathroom humour that appeals to the under seven-year-old, as well as the naughty post-pubescent in all of us. We may not want people to know that we are going to the loo but we crack jokes about it all the time.

Sequestered away from prying eyes, public restrooms can be places of solace where one can escape the pressures of co-workers, the harassment of school peers or avoid a socially uncomfortable moment at a restaurant dinner table. Their intimate nature allows for uninhibited self-expression, both social and sexual. For instance, graffiti isn't always humorous; it espouses social issues, frustrations and trends within a private space that creates awareness of controversial topics, not only for oneself but for others as well. A recent study of the content of graffiti in the restrooms of a female West Coast American university revealed that the most frequently occurring subjects after sex, relationships and drugs were politics, religion and cries for help which all registered significant percentages. Sexually, the domestic bathroom is the place where as children and teenagers we first explore our bodies safely locked away from the prying eyes of our parents, while public conveniences have long been associated with furtive intimate relations, especially among gay men who use stalls for casual sexual encounters and peepholes for anonymous fellatio.

Toilets are humble appliances yet they, and the spaces in which we use them, are microcosms of societies which vary from country to country. The negative values ascribed to excrement, connecting it to everything profane,

evil and detestable, are absent in some cultures where the human body and its products are not considered antithetical to the 'mind' and to social values. In pre-Hispanic Mexico, for example, excrement was conceived as powerful and ambivalent and scenes of defecation found their way into religious iconography. In Japan, traditional toilet culture viewed the restroom as a place of meditation and relaxation. In the 1933 essay 'In Praise of Shadows' Junichiro Tanizaki examined the textures and imagery of Japanese art, architecture and design and the important role that shadows played both physically and metaphorically in Japanese culture. He wrote: 'The parlour may have its charms, but the Japanese toilet truly is a place of spiritual repose. It always stands apart from the main building, at the end of a corridor in a grove fragrant with leaves and moss. No words can describe that sensation as one sits in the dim light, basking in the faint glow reflected from the *shoji*, lost in meditation or gazing out at the garden in a quiet so complete one can hear the hum of a mosquito.'

The Chinese have no qualms about their bodily functions; spitting in public is common and blowing your nose directly on the ground is acceptable. Until recently, when the country embarked on a programme of regeneration to prepare for the international visitors descending on the city of Beijing, the host of the 2008 Olympics, public conveniences were just that – very public. They consisted of a communal trough over which the user squatted along with any other patrons visiting the facility. Such a 'toilet' was the centrepiece of Fruit Chan's art-house movie *Public Toilet* (2002), a series of four loosely connected stories which revolve around lavatories and include graphic and uninhibited scenes of defecation.

Even in Euro-American cultures attitudes diverge. In the United States, where the repression of the natural and the need to separate the individual from his/her waste is probably greatest, there is still a resistance to accessories for washing the bottom after visiting the toilet and neither the French bidet nor the Japanese Toto toilet, which cleans and deodorizes its customer after every use, have traditionally attracted many patrons. In Germany, The Netherlands and Eastern Europe, toilets invariably consist of a bowl with a shelf on which faeces lie before they are flushed away. A practical and hygienic invention, it allows the user to examine the healthiness of their stools, and despite what you might think produces fewer obnoxious odours than the water bowl toilet, yet is viewed with an aversion bordering on fear by the Americans and British. US writer Erica Jong aggressively declares in her novel *Fear of Flying* (1973), 'I hated the Germans for always thinking about their damned stomachs, their Gesundheit … I hated their fanatical obsession with the illusion of cleanliness … a carefully contrived façade to intimidate foreigners with Germany's aggressive wholesomeness. But just go into any German toilet and you'll find a fixture unlike any other. It has a cute little porcelain platform for the shit to fall on so you can inspect it before it whirls off into the watery abyss.'

The design of any bathroom, both private and public, is therefore loaded. In our domestic environment we will go to no ends to eliminate

8

9

10

11

12

13

8 Bathroom graffiti or 'latrinalia' is a type of inscribed marking on restroom walls which can take the form of art, drawings or words. Often of a scatological nature, it forms a public reference to the taboo subject of bodily functions.

9 Toilet graffiti espouses controversial social issues. A recent survey of latrinalia found in a woman's restroom in the West Coast of America revealed that after humour, sex and drugs, the topics most visited were politics, religion and cries for help.

10 Will Rogers Memorial Park Restroom, Beverly Hills, California, where the undercover LAPD officer Marcelo Rodriguez arrested singer George Michael for lewd behaviour in 1998. Michael's arrest led to him being publicly outed as gay after years of mystery surrounding his sexuality. Later he released the single and video *Outside*, which poked fun at Rodriguez and was a deliberately satirical comment on the taboo of practising gay sex in public restrooms. In the video there are explicit scenes of male officers kissing and Michael dances in front of disco ball urinals dressed in the same officer's uniform.

11 The American TV series *Ally McBeal* starred Calista Flockhart as a young lawyer and focused on the romantic and personal lives of the main characters. The majority of the episodes included the unisex restroom as a centrepiece for trading gossip, bonding and bursting into song and dance routines, and did much to popularize the concept of communal facilities in offices.

12–13 The architectural artist Monica Bonvicini's *Don't Miss A Sec* exhibit (a useable public toilet enclosed in a one-way mirrored glass box) was installed on a building site across the road from London's Tate Britain in 2003. It addresses the concept of voyeurism and privacy by allowing the user to see out while passers-by cannot peep in. 'Playing with the idea of the most private bodily function and having to sit on a street corner is just bizarre,' says Jeff Boloten, who works at Tate Britain.

14 overleaf Fascinated by the way in which imagery hits the viewer sublimely, the British artist Mat Collishaw is known for his provocative video sculptures. The large-scale projection of a baby bathed in ultraviolet light is used in public restrooms to stop drug users locating their veins.

15 overleaf Toilets are embarrassing, not shocking. If an artist can out-shock the embarrassment, then he or she can succeed in elevating the spectator's mind from associations with excrement to the statement that he or she wishes to convey. This can be seen in *Fountain* (1917), the most famous of Marcel Duchamp's 'readymades', a conceptual piece which shifts the focus of art from physicality to interpretation.

their distasteful dimensions. We use extractor fans and perfumed sprays to get rid of bad odours, run taps to disguise unpleasant noises, crochet cloches to cover our prettily patterned and scented toilet rolls; the bathroom is a demonstration of good taste, often expensively fitted with the toilets, like the basins and baths, of cutting-edge design bearing the names of leading international architects and designers such as Karim Rashid, Ross Lovegrove, Philippe Starck, Marc Newson, Jean Nouvel, Stefano Giovannoni, Marcel Wanders and Jasper Morrison, all of whom have produced lines for leading bathroom manufacturers Roca-Laufen, Alessi, Ideal Standard, VitrA, Dornbracht and Duravit, to name but a few.

In the publc realm, the restroom is the most essential space in any public building but until relatively recently it has been the most undervalued; it has been treated as a necessary evil rather than a bountiful blessing. For decades these areas were largely ignored by the architect and his client who installed functional and hygienic rooms which may have followed the many manuals written on the subject of what constitutes a properly designed restroom in terms of health, safety, privacy and space allocation but with little attempt at being creative. Restrooms were efficient yet stood in aesthetic isolation from the interior for which they were intended. The economic boom of the 1980s saw entrepreneurs turning to design as a way of adding value to their businesses and distinguishing themselves from their competitors.

A clean, well-designed and innovative restroom feature can be a business tool for attracting customers to public places and, consequently, for increasing profitability. At present, yesterday's under-funded and virtually overlooked public facilities are benefiting from a growing and highly publicized interest in lifestyle and design, a trend that has led to the makeover of even the most functional of daily routines. The examples of restrooms contained in this book are well thought out and well funded spaces, which were conceived to offer an integrated design statement within the overall interior concept of a building.

The office restroom is becoming a selling point. Clean and efficient is no longer enough; as a three-dimensional marketing tool, the restroom should promote the company and be a memorable experience for employees, clients and visitors alike. Emanating from the United States and popularized by such cult TV programmes as *Ally McBeal*, the unisex restroom is now common and, like the ubiquitous break-out area in the twenty-first-century office, provides a space where workers can socialize and bond. In public venues and on the streets, restrooms have become less clinical and more spacious, affording perfumed retreats away from the madding crowd, while in bars and restaurants 'feature' lavatories are now prevalent. Using luxurious materials, rich surfaces, elegant fittings and finishes, and special effects, they are often entertaining talking-points announcing the quality of the establishment. Restaurateurs are increasingly aware that restrooms aren't just toilets but create an opportunity to develop an environment in which their clients can relax in a semi-public private space. Often with communal washrooms, they provide an area in which the

sexes can mingle, chat, powder and preen while getting to know one another.

Around the world designers are challenging the taboo that dictates precisely when, where, with whom and in what manner we go to the toilet; treading a fine line between the users' need for privacy as well as their social and psychological discomfort while recognizing the necessity to appeal to their emotions, intelligence and need for distraction. This book brings together 45 examples of restrooms which demonstrate that the ill-equipped and often dirty public facility is a thing of the past: using the toilet isn't just a physical pleasure but is often an entertaining and surprising one.

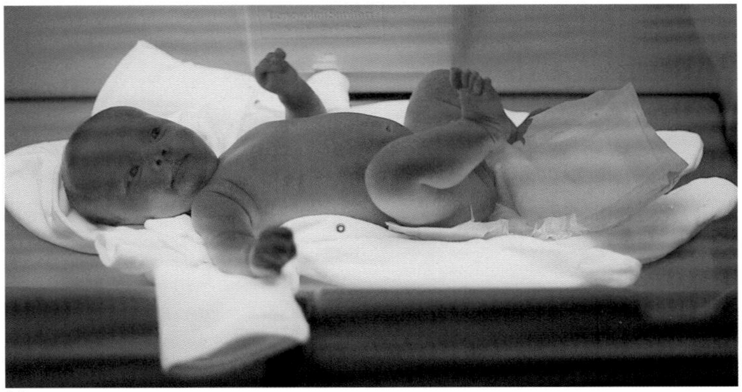

14

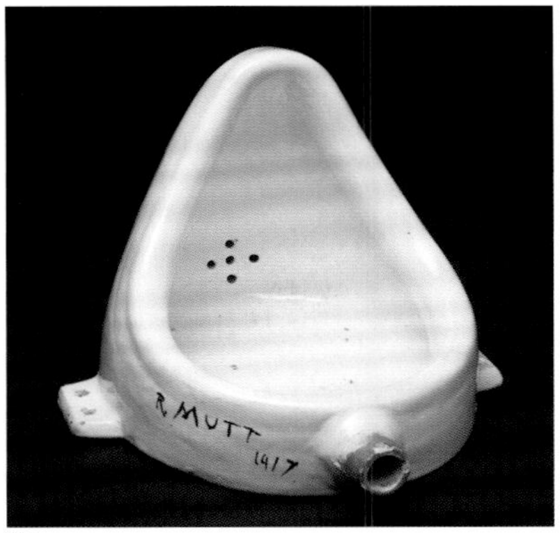

15

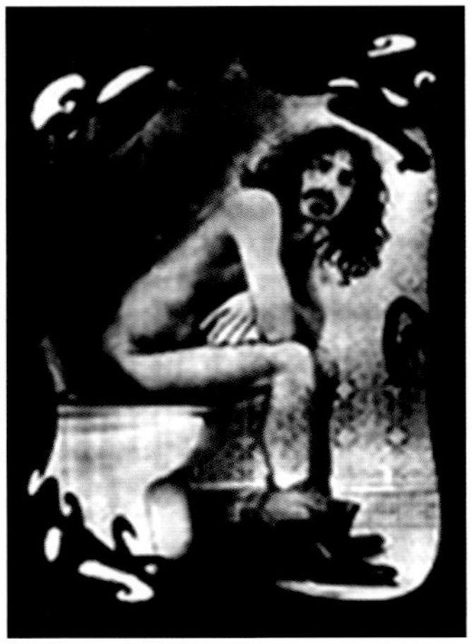

16

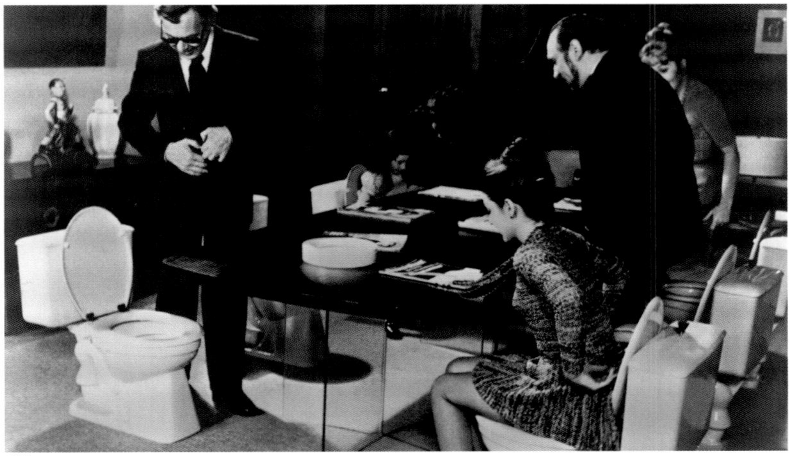

17

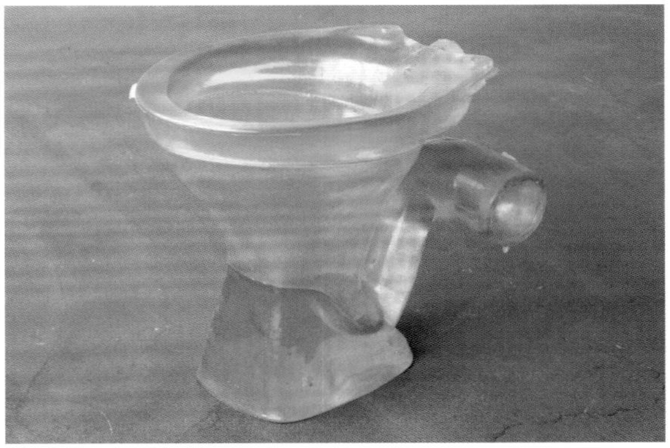

18

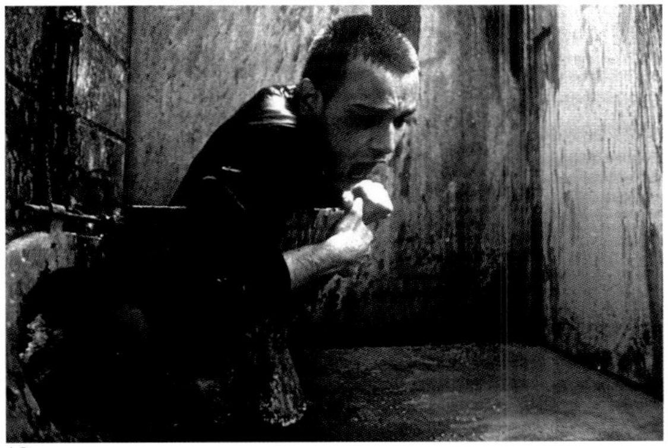

19

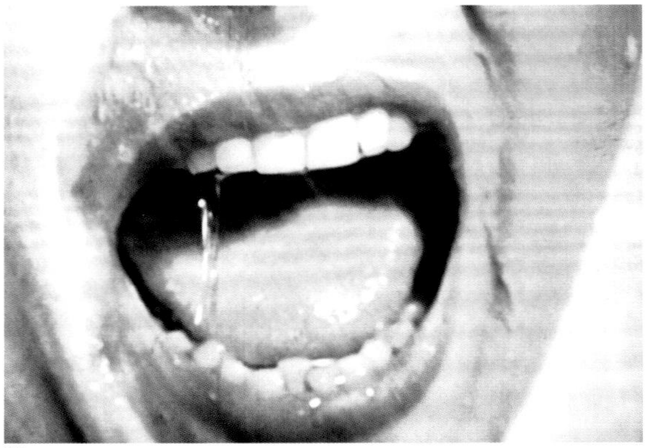

20

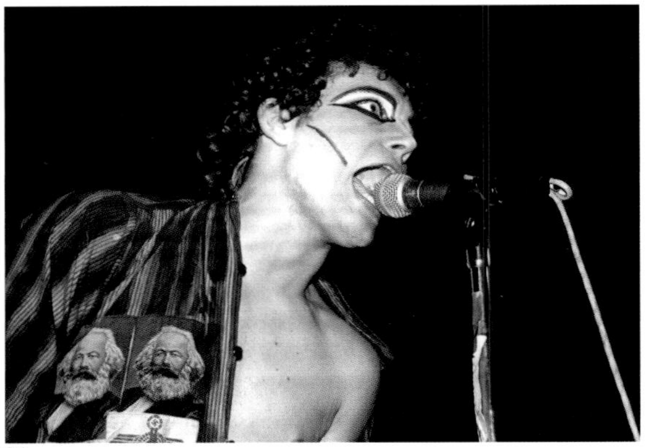

21

16 **The avant-garde rock star Frank Zappa (1940–94) influenced several generations with his radical and non-conformist music, as well as his battles against hypocrisy, censorship and social injustice. In the 1960s and 1970s, Zappa and his band, The Mothers of Invention, caused a furore in the United States with their dissonant attacks on society. Some of Zappa's anti-establishment lyrics revolved around toilet humour and thousands of his die-hard fans collected the infamous 1960s poster 'Phi Zappa Krappa', which shows him sitting naked on the toilet.**

17 **Luis Buñuel's *Le Fantôme de la Liberté* (1974) was his most surreal film, consisting of a series of episodes criticizing middle-class bourgeois mores. The most famous scene turns the taboo of bodily functions on its head by depicting a dinner party scene where people sit on toilets around the table but retire to little rooms to eat.**

18 **Britpack art can be characterized by its controversial content of a scatological or sexual nature. In *The Old in Out* (1998), Sarah Lucas presents nine coloured polyurethane toilet casts to pay homage to the work of fellow artist Rachel Whiteread. 'I like the shape of toilets … Everyone relies on them. People try to avoid looking at them but I think they're quite heroic,' says Lucas.**

19 **Danny Boyle's film *Trainspotting* (1996) addresses the problem of heroin addiction from both users' and anti-drug stances and has the ability to shock. In the 'Worst Toilet in Scotland' scene, Renton (played by Ewan McGregor) renounces drugs cold turkey but dives into a filthy toilet to retrieve his last hit – a pair of opium suppositories. Showing just how low a junkie will sink, Boyle's image has a far more powerful anti-drug message than any Reagan-era 'Just Say No' advertisement.**

20 ***Psycho* (1960) brought a toilet to the screen for the first time, breaking the United States' cinematic toilet taboo. Alfred Hitchcock had to fight the studio system to keep the scene of Janet Leigh flushing a piece of paper down the pan: 'This is where you are going to get to know what the human race is all about. We're going to start by showing you the toilet and it's only going to get worse' (Joseph Stephano, screenwriter on *Psycho*).**

21 **Punk's infatuation with the spontaneous, the dirty and the taboo, often including both toilet humour and frank asides to biological functions, resulted in a stripped-to-the-bone assault on the ears and eyes as well as the middle-class moral values of 1970s England. Scatological references, endorsing the trash aesthetic, became part of the lexicon. Although no major references were made to toilets in brand names, songs or slogans, there was an indirect allusion through acts such as Acme Sewage Co, the Snivelling Shits and Rudimentary Peni. In 1976, during his punk rock years, Stuart Leslie Goddard renamed himself as Adam Ant, after the urinal manufacturer (Adamant).**

Public
Conveniences

WC1
The Marchhare
London, UK

right
Exterior view of WC1. The first-ever boutique powder room for women is located in London's busiest shopping street and directly opposite the world-famous Selfridges department store. The brightly-lit façade signifies the luxury to be found inside.

opposite top
The aesthetic of the powder room is very 'girlie': white upon white with a touch of lush pink. A light Italian tiled floor and satin/pearl chandeliers from CTO Lighting add a touch of glamour.

opposite bottom
The Marchhare, business developer and designer, believe that, although restroom design has developed, maintenance and service has not been addressed. WC1 comes complete with an attendant selling a range of 'Rescue' products, offering the weary customer a quick make-over. Prices for using WC1 vary according to level of service, from basic use of the facility to pamper and then to full makeover.

WC1 gives a whole new meaning to the phrase 'spend a penny'. For the privilege of using this luxurious convenience the female shopper needs to flush a few pounds down the pan.

This public restroom at 439–441 Oxford Street, WC1, presents the opportunity to enter a spa-shop-toilet. Time will tell if the woman in the street will opt for the generic loo found in this busy central-London location or hand over the amount it would cost to buy body lotion for a week at WC1.

Nineteen spacious cubicles (cleaned after every use and freshened by five air changes a minute), as well as a spacious communal area replete with sofas, a range of scented beauty products and the soothing strains of lounge music, are tempting for the foot-weary. Yet is this alluring enough? WC1 is not located in the latest nightspot where women visit the restrooms to catch up on the latest gossip. It is in the middle of the busiest shopping street in London, where passers-by rarely stop for more than a moment to get rid of excess baggage.

The WC1, however, is part of a growing trend for luxury restrooms. POINTWC (see page 34) has recently opened in Paris – it's free, but certainly chic – and Charmin's branding experience in Times Square, New York, is anything but squalid. In this age when the six-star hotel is about to take over the hospitality industry and the super rich are prepared to pay £84 million ($116.2 million) for a flat overlooking Hyde Park, perhaps WC1 have got it right and the average female shopper will splash out for a little old-fashioned powder-room glamour.

WC1 provides hairdryers, straightening irons, toiletries and stalls that are roomy enough to change in. The

circular 'salon' has pebble walls, stone floors and a constant supply of fresh flowers and is spacious and superbly lit, with crystal chandeliers designed to flatter skin tones. Attendants are on hand to provide WC1's own range of 'Rescue' products, from stockings to sewing kits, and for an extra fee customers can also book neck and shoulder massages.

WC1 is the first in a series of boutique restrooms for women. With a further nine in the pipeline, it will be interesting to see whether the multi-million price tag will justify itself. Advertised as a revival of the Victorian powder-room, it is worth considering that perhaps twenty-first-century women no longer have the luxury of time that was enjoyed by their nineteenth-century counterparts.

left
Axonometric showing the layout of WC1. To maximize the small 372 square metre (4000 square foot) space, both the powder room and cubicles have a circular floor plan.

opposite top
The Marchhare compared designing the restroom area to building a small 20-bedroom hotel. Each cubicle is a room in its own right with VitrA sanitaryware and ambient lighting.

opposite bottom left
Mirrors are absent to encourage women to use the powder room. To avoid queuing, an electronic numbering system enables staff to control the flow of customers.

opposite bottom right
The cubicles are situated off a central atrium. Flowers, which are changed daily, and scented candles add to the luxurious ambience.

Hasuikebori
Akira Watanabe and Masahiro Ikeda
Tokyo, Japan

left
**The building opens
up towards the moat.
The slatted nature
of the non-structural
timber walls allows
natural ventilation.**

right
**The interior affords
views out onto the
Hasuikebori moat.
Lightness and
transparency is
maintained by the
use of large picture
windows and the
open slatted walls.
The taps are fitted
with infrared sensors
to control water
consumption.**

Hasuikebori translates as 'Lotus Pond' and this small but innovative piece of architecture stands next to the flower-filled moat separating the grounds of the Imperial Palace, closed to the general public for most of the year, from the East Garden, a popular place of relaxation for the inhabitants of Tokyo escaping the frenetic life of the metropolis.

The Palace is situated in the centre of Tokyo, a short walk from the main railway station, on land that was once occupied by the Edo Castle, home to the Tokugawa shogun, which ruled Japan from the seventeenth to the nineteenth centuries. The Hasuikebori pond is one of the original moats, which along with the massive ramparts, divided the outlying fortifications from the imperial residences.

Watanabe and Ikeda's design for the restrooms takes into account the special landscape of this location to preserve a taste of nature in the centre of the city. 'What I first paid attention to was the locale,' says Watanabe. 'Thinking about the Hasuikebori and the stone rampart that is visible across the moat, I wanted to avoid a building that would be intrusive.'

The architects' first idea was to create an umbrella-shaped construction, with a textile roof supported on one pillar which would allow air to flow freely through the transparent structure. Without losing sight of the original concept, but taking into consideration the monumental stone boundaries which announce the imposing imperial palaces beyond, this was translated into a design with a greater sense of stability. Taking advice from the shipping industry, the architects conceived a method of welding a pliable and lightweight aluminium roof to a steel structure. By employing a technique

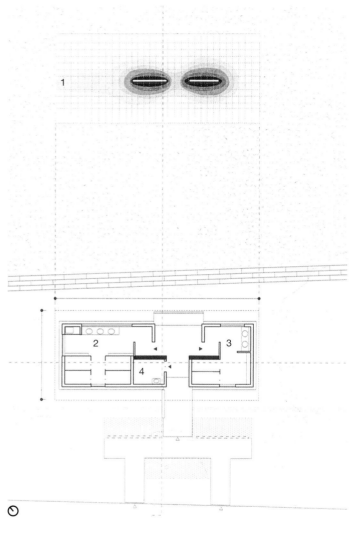

right
The interiors blend the coldness of the undulating aluminium roof and the cubicle dividers with the warmth of the wood panels dividing male and female spaces.

opposite left
Floor plan. Male and female spaces are clearly defined. Yet the common access point frames a view of the historical stone wall of the castle and the lotus pond, giving a shared experience for the users. 1 Moat 2 Female restroom 3 Male restroom 4 Disabled restroom

opposite right
View across the Hasuikebori moat towards the restrooms, which unobtrusively nestle in their surroundings.

known as 'explosion bonding', very rarely used in the construction industry, Watanabe and Ikeda developed a means of covering the entire structure by a roof supported on only one column with the walls acting as non-load bearing elements. The building tilts away from the flower-filled moat to give the impression of 'opening-up' towards the Hasuikebori, reinforcing the lightness and fluidity of the design. Serendipitously, the visibility of the bolts that were used to weld the aluminium gives the structure a sense of 'handiwork', mixing a high-tech with a low-tech aesthetic.

The interiors blend the coldness of the cubicle dividers and the aluminium roof with the warmth of the slatted timber walls. Up-lighters bounce light off the three-dimensional soffit, flooding the interior with a soft ambient luminescence. All fixtures and fittings are manufactured by Toto, including Japanese-style squatting toilets, self-cleaning urinals

and a face-saving sound device, which imitates the noise of running water.

The architects have developed new ways of exploring the expressive potential of aluminium within a 'social' context. 'We hope that this building will set some precedents,' concludes Ikeda.

Aire de Merle and Grans and Saint-Martin-de-Crau motorway
Béguin and Macchini
South of France

right
Night shot of the Aire de Merle convenience. Local stone has been used for the exterior, while the interior is clad in contrasting white tiles. Floodlights with a blue tint illuminate the white translucent canopy, which is umbrella-shaped to collect rainwater and aid the natural ventilation of the building.

opposite top
The section of the Aire de Merle restrooms shows the steel frame, which is hidden behind a tensile fabric covering, and descends to form a central core containing the toilets' technical plant.

opposite bottom
The floor plan illustrates the circular footprint of the restrooms. Access is made centrally, with male facilities to the left and female to the right. 1 Entrance 2 Male restrooms 3 Female restrooms

The 80 kilometre (50 mile) long A54 motorway speeds through the Provençal countryside between Salon-de-Provence and Nîmes, France, forming one leg of the journey linking Spain with Italy. It's a long haul for the 30,000 weary motorists who use the road daily but it has been enlivened recently by a series of tollbooths designed by Gilles Béguin and Jean-André Macchini. Alongside two of these tolls, the Parisian team have created restrooms. At Aire de Merle two buildings, one on each side of the road, are covered by tensile fabric structures, while next to the Grans and Saint-Martin-de-Crau toll plaza, four buildings are shaded by glass awnings. The varying forms of canopy, one soft and one hard, offer different methods of filtering the strong Mediterranean sunlight.

The concept behind the design for all the facilities was based on natural light (not surprisingly as it's the very same light which inspired artist Vincent van Gogh) and the architectural treatment had to be in tune with the vernacular of the

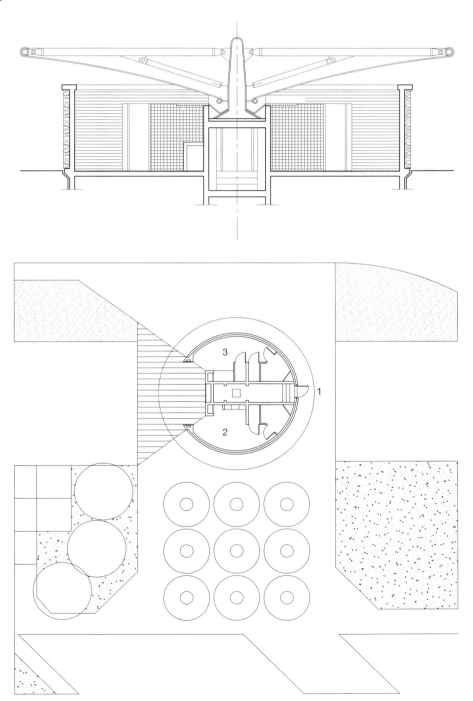

bottom left
The structure of the Grans and Saint-Martin-de-Crau restroom is covered by a glass roof. A protected aluminium brise soleil filters the strong Mediterranean sunlight.

bottom right
The interior is lined with shiny grey tiles. All materials, fixtures and fittings were selected for their durability and ease of maintenance.

opposite top
Local stone gives the ends of the building a rustic rough texture which contrasts with the central tiled core.

opposite bottom
The section (right) of the Grans and Saint-Martin-de-Crau restrooms shows the angled glass roof with brise soleil below. The floor plan (left) illustrates the symmetrical layout of the toilets with male and female facilities mirroring each other around the technical plant. 1 Female restroom 2 Female disabled restroom 3 Male restroom 4 Male disabled restroom 5 Urinals 6 Technical plant 7 Integrated wastebins

building materials found in this part of the country.

At Aire de Merle, the circular restrooms are accessible through a central opening. Exterior and interior have complementary textures. The outside is clad in rough local stone from La Crau while the inside is lined with shiny white tiles, chosen for their durability and ease of maintenance. The umbrella-shaped, translucent tensile roof stands clear of the walls and descends into a central core which houses the technical plant of the restrooms. At night, ground-placed floodlights shine up onto the white fabric and bounce off the tiled interior to produce a safety background lighting, which has the added advantage of giving these tiny gems an unearthly appearance.

The restrooms at Gran and Saint-Martin-de-Crau are accessed from either end, and stand next to the steel and glass tolls that stretch across the motorway. Natural stone and tiles have been used for the exterior and interior respectively, but in place of the organic aesthetic of a fabric canopy, a glass roof protected by an aluminium brise soleil forms an arbour covering the toilets. Floodlights are again placed in the ground circle and the building, creating a geographical marker along an otherwise unremarkable stretch of road.

The designs of all the facilities share a clean and brightly lit aesthetic which makes the user of these unmanned spaces feel secure. Male and female toilets are placed within the same structure, differentiated only by the graphics announcing each zone. The future will see restrooms conceived on the same model springing up along the length of the A54 motorway.

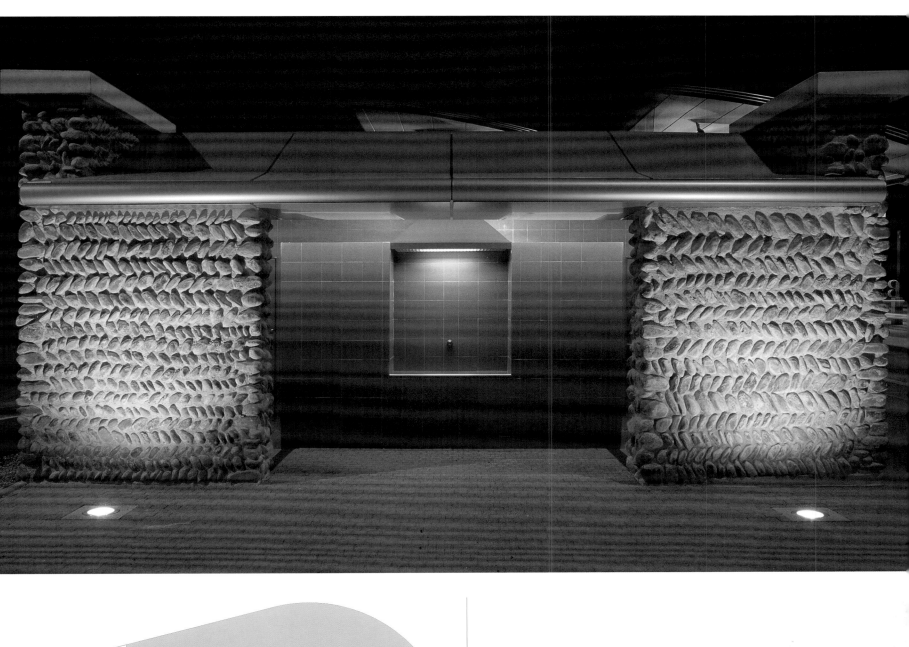

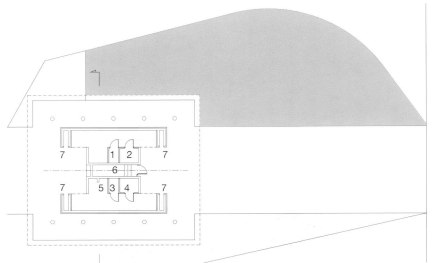

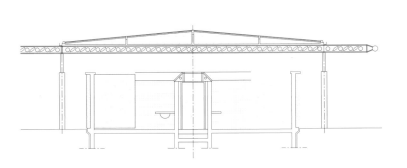

Urilift and UriGienic
Marco Schimmel, Urilift International BV
Various locations

If you have a fear of being buried alive then the Urilift and UriGienic are not for you. Dubbed the 'Tardis Toilet', these street urinals were invented by Dutchman Marco Schimmel to combat the annoyance caused by indiscriminate urination from party goers and clubbers once the pubs and nightclubs have closed. The added extra is that these innovative and unique capsules retract into the ground when no longer needed.

It could be argued that the provision of more public restrooms would be the natural answer to this unsavoury social problem, but they carry their own set of inconveniences. Quite often they are aesthetically unappealing, they have to be regularly monitored to guard against vandalism and graffiti, they are disliked by local residents and unfortunately are often used for purposes other than those for which they were intended – and, they are there all the time.

The Urilift, and its female equivalent the UriGienic, were conceived for 'nuisance' hotspots. They are only above ground when the demand is great. With the aid of a high-tech hydraulic system, the rest of the time the 2 metre (6 foot, 6 inch) high self-cleaning stainless-steel cylindrical structure sinks below the surface of the street and remains completely hidden; its roofs are available in 200 colours but can also be clad in the same surface material as the surrounding paving.

The Urilift has been carefully conceived so that three men can use it simultaneously without intruding on the privacy of each other. The UriGienic has a suspended toilet seat over a wok-like pan and returns automatically into an upright position when not in use, which makes it suitable for both male and female use. Both units are connected to the sewage system, electricity and water mains and, unlike mobile urinals, never need emptying. The levitating units are brightly lit, making them safe to use, and heated so they won't freeze over.

For those who are afraid, however, of sinking below ground without a trace, their minds can be put at rest: these futuristic time capsules that rise to the occasion of eliminating smelly alleyways may be periscopic but Urilift International have strict safety measures in place to ensure that no one will become stuck. The pop-up toilets can be operated with the touch of a button by the council, an attendant, the police force or by selected hotels, restaurants and bars, by an appointed operator who carries the unique control device, within a few metres of the unit.

left
The self-cleaning stainless-steel UriGienic has a clinical aesthetic. The toilet seat rises automatically when not in use.

opposite left to middle
The 2 metre (6 foot, 6 inch) high Urilift sinks into the ground during daylight hours when it is no longer needed.

opposite right
Once the unit is underground all that remains visible in the pavement is the circular cover, which is designed to withstand any weight and can be finished in vernacular paving for full integration within the street environment.

Multi-storey car park
Comprehensive Design Architects
Interior surface design by Paul Scott and Robert Drake
Workington, UK

Workington is an historic market town on the north-west coast of England with a long industrial heritage based around coal and iron-ore mining, iron working and steel making. In line with many such places, the late twentieth century brought a decline in Workington's traditional industries and the area suffered rural depopulation and neglect. The restrooms, located on Central Way underneath the new multi-storey car park, are part of a larger regeneration area. They have been funded by the Northwest Regional Development Agency at a cost of £2.74 million ($6 million), as part of a £4.5 million ($9 million) scheme to use local artists to improve public spaces in the new town centre development.

The projects also include a clock and a 9 metre (30 foot) sculpture made from resin and locally sourced granite in the town centre; glass canopies over the shop fronts in the Washington Square development; and the Hub, the town's centrepiece, with a three-dimensional

right
The Aquarium in the main entrance is the 'jewel in the crown' of the scheme and is stocked with local fish from the Solway.

bottom
Inside each cubicle door is one of a set of five texts entitled 'You Are Here', which set the reader's temporary location against wider contexts of geography, time and history.

opposite
Befitting the location of the restrooms underneath Workington's new multi-storey car park, fixtures and finishes can be easily cleaned and have a clinical, hygienic aesthetic.

You Are Here •

5500 miles from **Workington**
(Mashonaland East Province, Zimbabwe)
&
A long-haul flight from **Harrington**
(New South Wales, Australia)
&
An ocean apart from **Northside**
(Cape Breton Island, Canada)
&
Salterbeck, Mount Pleasant, South Carolina
Moss Bay, King County, Washington
&
Westfield, Orleans County, Vermont
Hamilton County, Indiana
Union County, New Jersey
Chautauqua County, New York
Hampden County, Massachussetts
&
Just a bus-ride from **Moorclose**, Rochdale
And **Stainburn**, Otley, West Yorkshire

soundscape, all managed by Allerdale Borough Council and Workington Regeneration in collaboration with Working pArts public art consultancy.

Ceramic artist Paul Scott, who has exhibited in Europe, North America and Australia (fittingly he curated a touring show, 'Are you Sitting Comfortably', which involved artworks on, in and made out of toilets) and Robert Drake, writer, stone waller and willow grower, were commissioned to develop designs for the tiles in this functional convenience. Drawing on the provenance, geographical location and associations of this largely forgotten but proud working-class town, their designs incorporate symbolic images and texts in a colour scheme (coal black, steel grey and iron red) inspired by West Cumbrian wagon cards. Photography was provided by Roger Lee.

There are three cycles of imagery within the restrooms: 'The Water Cycle', which describes the journey of water to

the site and runs horizontally along the walls of the female and male facilities; 'The History Line', floor-to-ceiling bands of text in the communal area near the entrance, each based on a famous person, place or event connected to Workington; and 'You are Here', which consists of facts relating to the world's 'Workingtons', located on the back of the restroom doors and above the hand driers, and in the baby changing and disabled facilities. An aquarium stocked with fish from the Solway was designed, built and is maintained by the Lake District Coast Aquarium, and situated in the entrance it underlines Workington's maritime location.

The Lake District, which lies just outside Workington, has a strong history of harnessing local talent to provide cultural enrichment. These restrooms are no exception.

THE LUCK OF WORKINGTON

Sunday 16th May 1568, about tea-time...
Mary, Queen of Scots, seeks refuge at Workington Hall after defeat of her forces in Scotland. She presents the Curwen Family ladies with a small agate drinking cup

The cup will bring good fortune
as long as it is not broken

1763 - the birth of Workington's Iron industry

Charcoal from southern Scotland
Iron Ore by packhorse from Frizington

BAREPOTTS MEADOW
NEAR HOLEGILL

• A mill for slitting and rolling bar iron
• A double forge for refining and drawing bar iron
• A foundry with several small furnaces
• A boring mill for boring cannon cylinders etc
• A grinding house and turning house and many other conveniences

left
Vertical bands of text, based on the shape of an old local railway ticket, narrate tales about people, events or places connected to Workington.

opposite
Texts and images decorating the tiles were designed by local artists Scott and Drake. In the main washroom areas of both male and female restrooms horizontal bands of text and illustration describe the journey of water to the site.

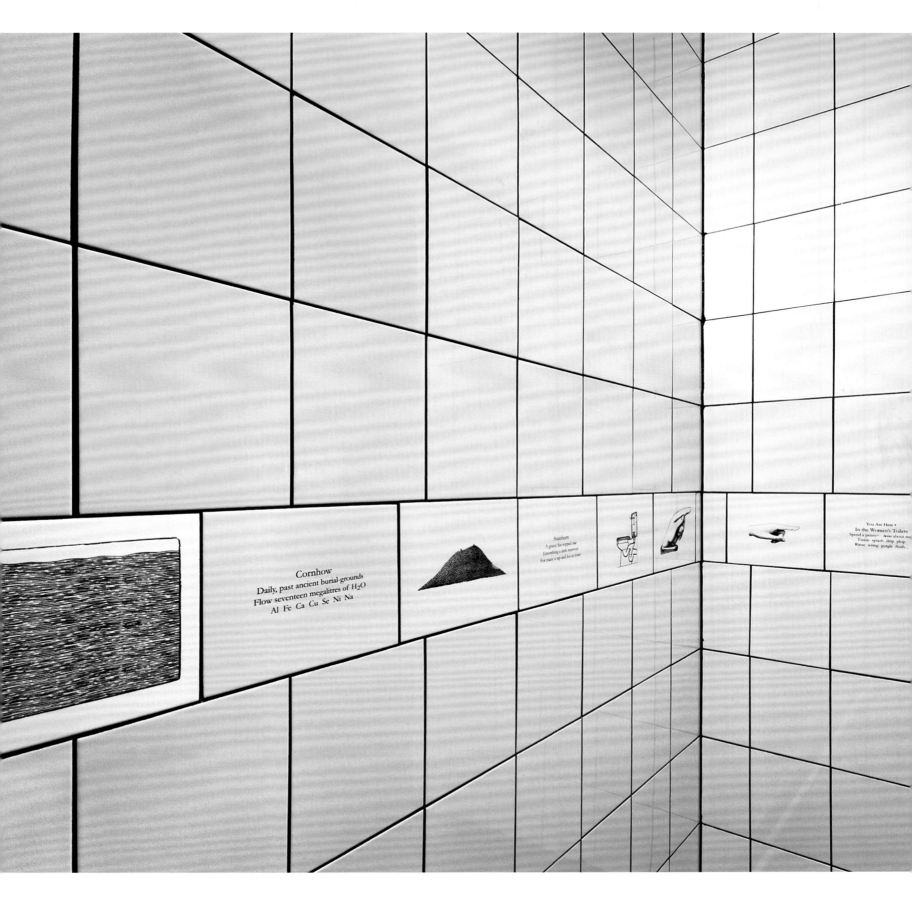

Cornhow
Daily, past ancient burial-grounds
Flow seventeen megalitres of H₂O
Al Fe Ca Cu Se Ni Na

Stainburn
A grainy flat-topped line
Entombing a dark reservoir
For many a tap and loo in town

You Are Here •
In the Women's Toilets
Spend a penny• twixt about me
Tinkle splash drip plop
Rinse wring gurgle flush...

City-Toilet 2=1
GK Sekkei
Berlin, Germany

GK Sekkei's City-Toilet 2=1 completes a line of interactive street furniture, commissioned and co-designed by the German corporation, Wall. With the motto 'Cleanliness starts with aesthetics', the manufacturing and outdoor advertising company invited leading international architects to work on concepts. Previous designers have included Professor Josef Paul Kleihues and Antonio Citterio. The range includes toilets suitable for disabled patrons, bus shelters, kiosks, city information facilities and guiding systems for tourists, all of which combine elegance with contemporary functionality. The brief demanded service points which fit comfortably within any environment by not being over-designed or too idiosyncratic. Hans Wall, previous Chairman of the Wall AG Brand, explained, 'We offer large cities tailor-made and future orientated products which blend harmoniously into every cityscape.'

Part of GK Sekkei's 'Intelligent Series', the 2=1's understated, clean geometric form is unremarkable. However, it's what this little box contains that is so innovative: the structure provides two separate booths in one and can be converted into a disabled toilet in a matter of seconds when the need arises. The restroom has both the extra space required by the physically impaired but it is also small and unobtrusive. High-quality materials, such as aluminium, stainless steel and matt, back-lit safety glass have been used, in order to cut down on the possibility of vandalism and graffiti.

The originality of the design lies around a flexible partition that, when extracted, automatically converts the two cubicles into a single large space. When the disabled person opens the door with a Euro key (obtained from the county council social services department), the panel separating the area vanishes into the rear wall, leaving two toilet bowls which can be accessed with a wheelchair from either side. The toilet has a swivel mechanism to provide the required space

and the user selects the position of the toilet before entering the cubicle. Once empty, the automatic cleaning device comes into play, disinfecting and drying the floor and toilet in 55 seconds. Then, the dividing wall re-appears, allowing the facility to be used once again by two separate patrons. Non-disabled people access the restroom by placing the appropriate coins in an exterior mechanism, which does not send out signals to the interior to convert. User time is limited to 20 minutes for regular patrons and 40 minutes for those with impaired mobility.

All the products developed for public spaces by Wall are self-financing. Using the revenue from advertising means that the city does not have to pay for maintenance or cleaning. Germanic efficiency and organization combined with international cutting-edge design means that the City-Toilet 2=1 is well and truly 'Für Städte. Für Menschen' ('For cities. For people'): the second of Wall's mottos.

The sequence of CADs illustrates how the flexible dividing panel retracts into the rear wall when the cubicle needs to be converted for the use of disabled people. A secure folding panel divides the space into two separate sections. The divider panel retracts and the washbasin folds up. Wheelchair users can access the toilet from the left or right side.

Professor Kleihues was the first to design 'street architecture' for Wall in 1997. His Streetline concept is based on a streamlined geometric figure: the spherical triangle. The form allows pedestrian traffic to circulate smoothly around the object on the sidewalk.

The Monbijou range of street furniture was developed by Antonio Citterio in 2003. The toilet is made from galvanized steel with a protruding powder-coated aluminium roof and transparent glass advertising panels. The design is characterized by its light, almost weightless form.

POINTWC
Nina Virus, Studio5491
Paris, France

right
Customers of
POINTWC are
welcomed by an
attendant who
ensures that the
stalls are cleaned
after each use and is
also on hand to sell
a range of gifts and
toiletries from the
restroom's boutique.

far right
Floor plan showing
the layout of the
restrooms. A large
entrance allows
for the boutique,
a play area for
children and easy
access for people in
wheelchairs.
1 **Entrance** 2 **Male
restroom** 3 **Female
restroom** 4 **Disabled
restroom**

opposite
The male (left)
and female
(right) restrooms
have different
atmospheres. The
heavy wood finish
and subdued but rich
colour scheme of the
former is reminiscent
of an Englishman's
club, whereas the
aesthetic in the
latter promises a
twenty-first-century
reworking of the
powder-room/boudoir
concept.

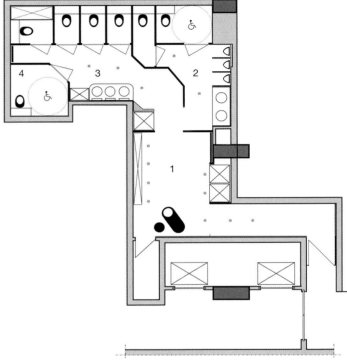

The POINTWC is located on the Champs-Elysées, a mecca for the fashionable. Here, the trend for luxurious public restroom spaces, which saw the launch of WC1 in London (see page 14), continues in Paris. However, for the indulgence of using this up-market facility you do not have to part with a princely sum, as in the case for its UK counterpart; a mere 1 euro will allow you into a world of scented opulence far from the madding crowd.

POINTWC is a branding exercise for Roca-Laufen, a manufacturer of sanitaryware and tiles, and as such is highly subsidized. It is also a great opportunity for what is known as 'tryadvertising'. Upon entering, customers are greeted by a smartly dressed bathroom attendant who sells products from a boutique shop, ranging from diapers to designer toilet paper-holders. Although only collaborating with Roca-Laufen at present, POINTWC intends to open a series of outlets throughout France and abroad: the director is also seeking to distribute samples of skincare brands in collaboration with major names such as Estée Lauder, Nivea and Clarins.

The designer of the restroom is Nina Virus, whose company Studio5491 specializes in communications and graphics. Also involved in product and interior design, the studio was ideally placed to deliver a proposal which would not only serve the needs of the public but would also offer what was required to subtly promote the brand of Roca-Laufen.

Nina Virus believes that as a society we are becoming evermore nomadic with daily routines of work, family, leisure and social life blurring into one, interrupted only by small breaks in public places. In this frenetic world, the primary need of visiting the bathroom is overlooked. The

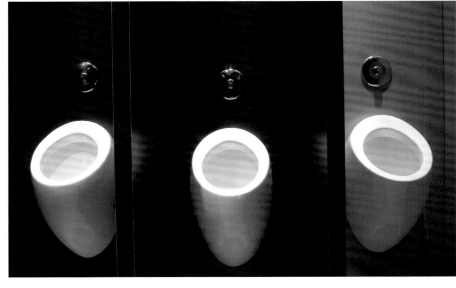

POINTWC is an attractive alternative to the often uncongenial public restrooms found in big cities. Her concept was to design an environment accessible to all, including children and the disabled, which provides hygiene, repose and a beauty break all under one roof. Taking creativity as the key word, she has dispensed with the often clinical aesthetic associated with public toilet design and conceived an artistic and 'trendy' space. While allowing for the fact that a facility such as this needs to be functional and easily maintained, she has played with a range of materials, colours and atmospheres to produce a setting which she describes as a 'home from home'. Each stall has a singular ambience with themes that vary from classic chic and ethnic to Zen and high-tech. The male and female zones are clearly differentiated: the former is described as an English Club and the latter as a twenty-first century boudoir.

While London's WC1 cost £1 million ($2 million) to build, an amount reflected in its higher entrance fee, POINTWC was designed on a limited budget. Studio5491 has used this to their advantage by employing simple and inexpensive materials to creative effect.

Lighting and graphics change according to the different spaces that guide clients through the different zones: welcome, shop (pictured) and stalls.

opposite
The stalls are given separate ambiences. Toilets and urinals are changed regularly to present the new product ranges of Roca-Laufen. Lighting in various colours has been used to create a pleasant and restful atmosphere.

Osaka Castle Park
Shuhei Endo Architect Institute
Osaka, Japan

In stark contrast to the constructed cityscape of Osaka, the Castle Park is one of the few places in the city where locals can escape their dense urban environment in search of relaxation among the trees and parkland of this historic attraction.

Shuhei Endo was given the commission to design a series of three public pavilions for the site: Halftecture OR, the largest and most significant housing a café, as well as male, female and disabled amenities, and two auxiliary restroom blocks, Halftecture OO and OJ.

These small buildings continue Endo's development of alternative building types named after one of their characteristics. Previous examples of this 'endotecture' have included the neologisms Springtecture, Rooftecture, Skintecture, Slowtecture and Bubbletecture, all of which challenge the authority and uniformity of modernist architecture defined by post, beam, roof and wall. Endo explains that 'my architecture is not one of point and line, but of original thought'.

Blurring the boundaries between interior and exterior, Halftecture is distinguished by its open aesthetic which incorporates views through all spaces. Endo believes that, while public restrooms are required to provide convenience, a feeling of ease can only be based on the openness and security derived from the clever handling of enclosure and privacy. OR is conceived as a circular floor plan with the café and restrooms placed around a central courtyard.

left
Halftecture OR is based on a circular floor plan around a central courtyard. The café is fully glazed, while the walls of the restrooms are clad in porcelain enamel.

bottom
The restroom and café pavilion have views across the moat to Osaka Castle. The rusty colour of the Cor-ten steel roof blends with the environment.

The form was selected to maintain the view to the castle, and the structure kept low to make the most of the surrounding bucolic environment. While the café is glazed, the walls of the restrooms are clad in porcelain enamel. The roof, made from 19 millimetre (0.75 inch) Cor-ten steel, is supported on sets of three slanting columns and appears to float above the main structure. A gap between the stalls and roof plays on the notion of concealment and exposure.

The two peripheral restroom blocks, OJ and OO, are rectangular in plan and have been covered in steel sheet metal, rusted to blend into its setting. As with OR the curved roofs stand independent of the walls, the former propped on the sloping end walls and the latter slung between two supporting A-frames. With his trilogy of small buildings, Endo proposes a new architectural statement in which the natural force of gravity is aesthetically incorporated into the structure rather than denied in the conventional way. Internally, the selection of the sanitaryware, fixtures and finishes was based upon the creation of a clinical aesthetic with durability and ease of maintenance in mind.

The Osaka pavilions demonstrate that even restrooms can become landmark buildings, redefining what we have now come to expect from contemporary modernist architecture.

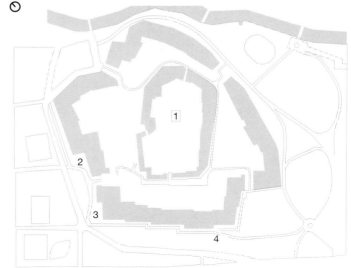

top right
Halftecture OO blends into its environment due to its specially rusted roof. Supported on two A-frames, it sags in the middle and was designed to look as though gravity is taking its toll.

centre right
The curve of Halftecture OJ's roof is created through hanging it from the 36 millimetre (1.4 inch) thick steel walls.

bottom right
Springtecture H, Sungu-cho, Hyogo, 1998. The structure of Endo's earlier restroom design takes the form of an independent spiral of corrugated steel sheets. Interior and exterior blend as the 'ribbon' twists and curls. The name derives from the building's tension and suggests a dynamic ability to spring.

opposite top
The ringed roof of Halftecture OR 'floats' above the main building, supported on tripods of 70 millimetre (2.8 inch) slanting columns. The sanitaryware is state of the art and manufactured by Toto. Finishes were selected for their clinical appeal and ease of maintenance.

opposite bottom
Site plan showing the position of the restroom blocks in relation to one another. 1 Osaka Castle 2 Halftecture OO 3 Halftecture OR 4 Halftecture OJ

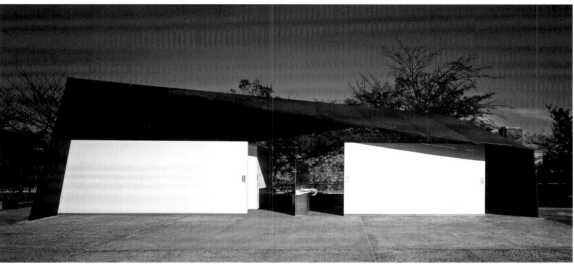

02
Public Venues

Museum of Applied Arts Café
Eichinger oder Knechtl
Vienna, Austria

left
The restrooms are located in the 'extra room', which is used as a lounging area. Childlike pastel shades have been used throughout. Curved, illuminated partitions contain private booths.

opposite top left
Surfaces are made from shiny HPL plastic panels or mirrored to reflect the light.

opposite top right
The sinuous stalls create a natural flow, maximizing a restricted space.

opposite bottom
The water of the specially created wash table flows from an internal source rather than from ordinary taps.

The refurbishment of the café of the Museum of Applied Arts was carried out as a collaboration by businessman Wolfgang Rosam, celebrity chef Helmut Ostereicher and architects Eichinger oder Knechtl, whose plan it is to open a series of cafés in various cities throughout Austria based on the traditional design of the *gasthaus*.

Austria is historically associated with café-culture, yet Eichinger oder Knechtl insist that the *gasthaus* is a much wider phenomenon. More in common with the relaxed atmosphere found in a German beer cellar than the refined ambience of

Belle Epoque coffee houses, the plan of such establishments is tripartite with distinct bar and dining areas and an *extrazimmer* (literally 'extra room'), which all flow seamlessly together.

The former café was unremarkable and had not been operating to capacity for some time. The director of the museum, Peter Noever, specified a brief for a design that would blend the traditional with the experimental. The architects had already worked on the interiors of a number of rooms in the museum so were in tune with the essentials of his philosophy.

The bar is dominated by the ornate plasterwork of the original building, which

the architects gave a contemporary look by inserting a 22 metre (72 foot) long mirrored 'light sail' that geometrically bends and folds across the entire length of the room and is punctuated by a chandelier made from wine bottles suspended above the bar. The dining room is a more sober affair and illustrates the traditional *gasthaus* atmosphere. Perforated wooden panels are back-lit in pastel tones which run up one wall and across the acanthus moulding of the ceiling, unifying and giving an intimate feel to what would otherwise be a rather intimidating large room.

The restroom (both male and female toilets are located in one space and

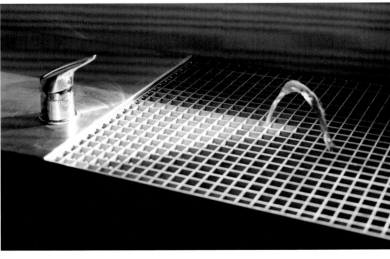

colour-coded; blue for the men and pink for women) is located in the basement of the 'extra room', which is used for lounging and drinking and housed in a zig-zag, bronze-clad pavilion in the inner courtyard. Eichinger and Knechtl wanted the restrooms to echo the concept of this cosy yet contemporary adjunct to the main space. The colour scheme is bold and simple, which reflects the almost child-like palette of apple green, raspberry red and sunshine yellow used in the upholstered seating of the room above. The cubicles are coiled and sinuous. The architects refer to the concept as 'infinity design'. Maximizing the floor area by making a simple traffic-flow plan, which loops and bends back on itself, gives a feeling of space and luxury in a restricted area. The stalls also mimic the curved illuminated partitions, which screen the seating booths within the 'extra room'. The urinals and toilets are simple but were selected for their elongated forms, which add a vertical accent that makes the space appear larger. As there is no natural illumination, the lighting plan was important. Strips outline the mirrors;

reflections bounce off the shiny High Pressure Laminate (HPL) plastic surfaces of the cubicles. A custom-made 'sink' features a water source that is located from within, what looks like, a tabletop, adding an innovative element to the functional sanitaryware.

The key element to the design of this *gasthaus* is a sequence of spaces from the solidity of the bar to the elegance of the pavilion. The restrooms follow the same natural flow and reflect the overall concept of the café.

bottom
Rendering showing the unisex restroom cubicles, delineated by blue for men and pink for women.

opposite
Sanitaryware was selected for its elongated form, again creating a vertical accent making a small area seem larger. Lighting has the same effect and was also important in a basement location without natural light.

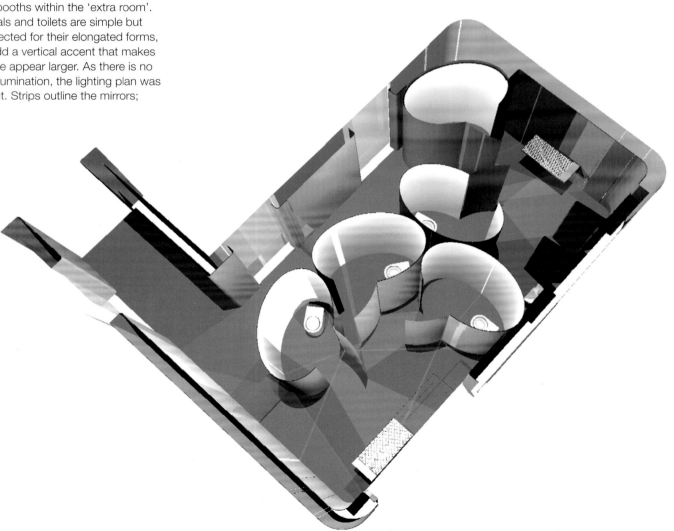

'Belle et Fou' Theatre
Meuser Architekten BDA
Berlin, Germany

The design of the 'Belle et Fou' Theatre pays homage to the decadent days of the speciality theatre in 1920s Germany. Liberated from decades of oppressive imperial rule by the First World War and the abdication of Emperor Kaiser Wilhelm II, a defeated populace enjoyed a sexually-charged permissive nightlife in venues dedicated to drinking and sensuality. Actors and audience mingled in subterranean interiors that blurred the boundaries between acting, dancing and cabaret in a devil-may-care attitude. They revelled the night away to spill out onto the shattered streets of Berlin as dawn was breaking. This Weimar decadence is captured in the Neue Sachlichkeit (New Objectivity) paintings of Georg Grosz and Otto Dix, and inhabited by Sally Bowles in her bowler hat and suspenders. They symbolize a brief moment of emancipation before the Third Reich stamped their clean, ethnic control on any form of personal expression.

The 'Belle et Fou' Theatre re-visits this sub-genre of theatrical entertainment in a luxurious and sensual space which mixes eating, theatre and dancing under one

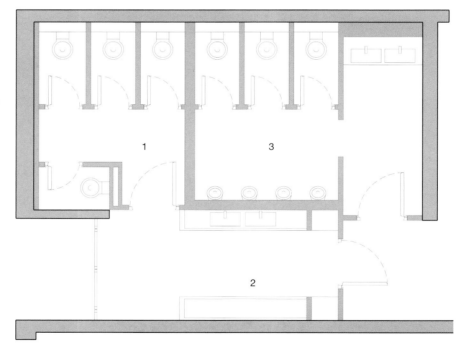

top left
Shot of the main auditorium. Although the traditional separation between stage and seating has been maintained, barriers between actors and audience have been broken down in a space where artists and spectators mingle.

bottom left
Floor plan of the restrooms. By law in Germany the male and female zones have to be separate in public places. Conceptually the areas are identical.
1 Female restroom
2 Female make-up area 3 Male restroom

opposite
The entrance to the female restroom has a full-length make-up bench, surmounted by an ornate baroque mirror that produces infinity reflections in the mirror above the sinks opposite. Diffuse ambient lighting is offset by the custom-made chandelier by Dutch designers Brand van Egmond.

bottom
Aerial view of the feature sink. A panel incised with a floral pattern reminiscent of the rich decoration typical of oriental architecture is fixed over the sink.

opposite
The cubicles are kept simple with elegant Alessi-designed, Roca-Laufen toilet pans which highlight the opulent design of the communal spaces.

roof. The Berlin-based architects Philipp and Natascha Meuser won a competition to re-build a storey of the new theatre in the Spielbank Berlin, part of the regeneration of Potsdamer Platz. The area with its bars and restaurants, cinemas, music halls and casino was an ideal location in which to reinvent the concept of the speciality theatre. In collaboration with the theatrical producer Hans-Peter Wodarz and artistic director Arthur Castro, the Meusers have combined architectural and stage art to create a unique environment which eschews the middle-class cultural canon of theatrical design. Although the stage has been traditionally separated from the semicircle of the audience level, the architects have created an intimate ambience, where the artists and spectators practically rub shoulders with one another.

The male and female restrooms (in Germany there have to be separate facilities in public places) were designed with the same architectural care as their surroundings, and in keeping with the voluptuous interiors of the theatre. This was an ideal chance for the Meusers to be as creative as possible, using light, space and materials to the limits of their expressive capacities. The restrooms are conceived in the same opulent manner as the auditorium, bar and restaurant, encouraging visitors to feel that they too are on stage. Exquisite details act as theatrical 'props': the eye-catching floral sink panel through which the water drains away, and the baroque mirror over the make-up bench combine with artful lighting in the form of a custom-made chandelier by Dutch designers Brand van Egmond and diffuse down-lighters over the basins and preparation areas.

The 'Belle et Fou' Theatre is a place where one views and is viewed. It features an experiential environment dedicated to self-expression, and the restrooms are designed with the same philosophy.

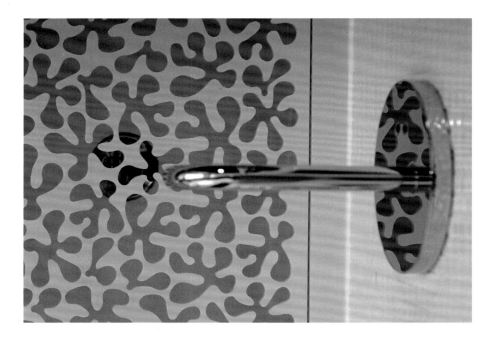

Crèche
RCR Aranda Pigem Vilalta Arquitectes
Manlleu, Spain

left
The restrooms are situated off a corridor in the central zone of the building. The lime green, cherry red and tangerine orange of the glass façade have been repeated in the Plexiglas structures, which divide the space.

opposite
Vibrant lollipop colours have been used to soften the minimalist lines of the crèche and make them playful.

Although they rarely work outside the Catalan province of Gerona in the north-east of Spain, RCR Arquitectes have built up a wide reputation for their unique interpretation of international modernism. Their commissions generally come from the towns and villages surrounding Olot, where the practice is based, but their work cannot be accused of being regionalist. They have an easily recognizable style, defined by the use of repeated minimalist forms, interconnecting cubic volumes and a limited palette of materials (often glass, concrete and steel), which has attracted media and professional attention from around the world.

The severity of their normal approach made them an unusual choice of architect to design the Crèche at Manlleu, which lies 40 kilometres (25 miles) from Olot and 80 kilometres (50 miles) from Barcelona. However, the result bears witness to why this young practice has received such success since being formed in 1988. Undeniably minimalist, with a signature use of repetition and the linking of boxy pavilions, the partners Rafael Aranda, Carme Pigem and Ramon Vilalta have created a Lilliputian world of colour and enchantment geared towards the needs of babies and toddlers, but without losing sight of their trademark style.

What RCR have managed to create is a playful translation of modernism, based on the design of children's building blocks, with vibrant sweet-shop colours as the defining element. Light floods into the nine playrooms through glass plates of alternating lime green, cherry red and tangerine orange. To better understand the building, one should view it on hands and knees. Sight lines have been

designed at a child's eye level and the entrance itself is dominated by a hanging, coloured element, which the children can pass freely beneath, but has to be skirted by accompanying adults.

A central zone houses cupboard space, a washing area and the toilets. The same lollipop colours are repeated in bright Plexiglass structures, which are enhanced by the light that falls through skylights and washes the space with rainbow hues. Providing toilets for children under the age of three is a huge responsibility. The major issue at this stage is toilet training – the child has to learn to control his or her bodily needs, which if successfully achieved leads to a sense of accomplishment and independence. In designing a friendly, transparent, bright and colourful area, with all fittings including the actual toilet pans at the toddlers' level – and partitions just high enough to afford a degree of privacy without shutting the children off from what is going on around them – RCR have created a safe and unthreatening environment. This is far removed from the sterile, white, doorless cubicles, reeking of disinfectant, which have intimidated many generations of infants.

left
The interiors have been designed with the needs of the infant uppermost. Site lines are on a child's eye level and the toilets appear Lilliputian. The semi-open/closed toilet partitions afford a degree of privacy while allowing the user to still be part of what is going on around them.

Artoteek refurbishment
Renovation by NEXT Architects
Restroom tile design by Ica van Tongeren
The Hague, The Netherlands

This small restroom is a glowing example of how art and craft can be employed to lend an otherwise unremarkable space a sense of cultural identity.

Housed in an historical building in the Dutch capital The Hague, Artoteek is an art gallery/business devoted to the promotion of art within the community. An 'Artbank' allows customers to borrow paintings much as a book can be taken from a library for a period of time. Primarily, the concern is commercial and this is reflected in NEXT Architects' refurbishment in which the interiors have been kept white, clean and modest. However, for the restroom the architects wanted a total contrast. The opportunity presented itself to turn an unobtrusive, functional room into art itself, to create a talking point for visitors. In NEXT's brief to the Dutch ceramicist Ica van Tongeren, who they employed to work up the existing tiles, they asked for a design which would make people say: 'Have

you been to the bathroom yet? That was an experience.' The client asked for the antique wash-bowl and cistern to be preserved, but otherwise the architects had carte blanche.

Van Tongeren has been exploring how to apply innovative techniques in photography to tile design since her final exam at the Gerrit Rietveld Acadamie. Believing that decoration is a means of preserving the past, she has collaborated on numerous occasions with the Royal Delft Porcelain Factory, where the traditional Delft Blue is still made.

For Artoteek, van Tongeren developed a concept for the tiles based on their original *fleur de lis* design, enhancing the old with a new motif. The ceramicist used Delft colouring, which she believes evokes a sense of history and speaks directly to the emotions of the Dutch. Adopting modern technology, through a combination of photography, digital manipulation and high-temperature fired transfers, she made the coat of arms of The Hague, a stork with an eel in its beak, into the decoration for the tiles. A special glazing process resulted in the pattern taking on the classic Delft hue to become a permanent part of the tile. The stork is depicted in its actual size at floor level but reduces in scale as the detail is repeated towards the ceiling. The perspective gives the tiny cubicle a sense of space.

By elegantly using photography to enhance traditional ornament, van Tongeren has created a modern resurrection of classic imagery. 'Often in the case of a renovation, it's out with the old and in with the new, even though elements from the past go quite well with new additions,' she reflects.

De Effenaar backstage restrooms
Bob Copray and Anthony Kleinepier
Eindhoven, The Netherlands

left
**All non-architectural
parts of the interiors,
such as counters,
bars, coat-check
and box office,
were designed to be
integrated into the
architecture to give
the rooms a 'strong
character'.**

opposite
**The dressing room
toilets have been
given separate
identities through the
employment of strong
primary colours.
DD lacquer has been
used in the cut-outs
of the formwork units,
which contain the
washbasin and mirror.**

**De Effenaar is iconic in Dutch pop
culture. It was originally built as
a youth centre in the early 1970s
and quickly became the venue for
punk concerts. From its alternative
beginnings this 'pop mecca' gradually
developed towards the mainstream
while keeping its reputation as a
centre of subculture. The need for
a second auditorium, and the fact
that a subterranean river was slowly
eroding the foundations, resulted in
the search for an alternative site
to relocate this important piece of
Dutch cultural history.**

MVRDV's new De Effenaar is a bunker-like
concrete cube, which gathers secondary
rooms around a main concert hall. It
features a second performance space,
and a foyer, cloakroom, café and kitchen,
which are located at ground floor level,
with backstage, technical and performers'
foyer at the short sides of the building.
Achieving the impossible, MVRDV has
managed to create a structure which is
at once aesthetically sophisticated while
maintaining a raw, 'underground' edge.

Bob Copray and Anthony Kleinepier,
who were commissioned to bring a
local flavour to the project, conceived
all the non-architectural aspects of the
interiors. Copray was previously director
of Copray & Sholten, a young Dutch
practice which has built up a reputation
for working between the boundaries
of art and design. Kleinepier describes
himself as multi-disciplinarian. He
graduated as a product designer but, like
Copray, operates on the fringes between
the concrete and the abstract. Their
interventions included counters, bars,
coat-check, box office and dressing-
room toilets – free-standing units which
as Kleinepier points out, 'are meant to be
integrated into the architecture to give the
rooms a strong character'.

The dressing rooms house the
performers' toilets. The whole area was
designed to accommodate the inevitable

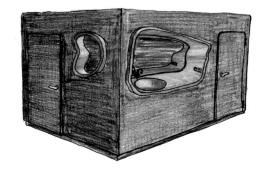

top left
All sanitaryware is standard so it can be replaced when it is vandalized.

top right
The cubicle interiors are finished in clear epoxy over meranti wood to protect it against graffiti.

opposite top
The cubicles which house the toilet and shower have a cell-like aesthetic, forming a room within a room.

opposite bottom
Sketches of the four restroom cubicles to be found in each of the four dressing rooms backstage.

vandalism which accompanies the kinds of bands previewing at the venue. 'The performers are often worse than the audience,' says De Effenaar's Director, Marijke Appelboom. 'They really trash the place.' The furniture, made by 24H Living in untreated pine, was designed specifically for artists to be able to leave their trace, while the toilets have been created to prevent any such defacement.

There are four dressing rooms altogether and each has been given a different ambience by using strong colours: blue, yellow, red and green. Normally backstage areas are plain and ordinary but Copray and Kleinepier believed that if they designed something special the bands would be surprised and less likely to leave the place damaged. The restrooms, which enclose a toilet and shower, stand independent from the infrastructure and form a room within a room. Built from dark brown formwork

panels incised with a coloured cut-out containing the washbasin and mirror, the units are vandal-proof. The interiors are finished in clear epoxy over meranti wood, which repels graffiti, while the formwork panels are slotted together without the use of screws to discourage their dismantlement. Although the box-like cubicles have a penitentiary feel, they are softened by the use of colour, and are both comfortable and practical.

Office of the Children's Commissioner
Feilden + Mawson
London, UK

The Office of the Children's Commissioner (OCC) was set up in 2006 as an independent foundation to encourage and support the voice of the child. With more than 11 million children in the UK, few organizations existed where the next generation could go to get help with issues such as bullying, antisocial behaviour, discrimination and disability.

The newly formulated OCC sought offices at No.1 London Bridge and commissioned Feilden + Mawson to design a set of spaces that would stimulate children to interact and talk about their problems, and which would also be appealing for adults. The result is a brightly coloured set of rooms, with soft curves, warm lighting and inflatable furnishings. The brief reflected the raison d'être of the OCC. Lisa White, Director of Communications, explains this approach: 'Our aim is to reveal the issues through information we gain from the children and young people themselves. Many of the children visiting the premises may be disabled or distressed, so the ambience of this workspace is crucial to enable communication.'

The concept for the restroom continues the theme of the rest of the interior. The client was open to all suggestions and the only limitations placed on the design were the normal restrictions concerning usability and technical issues. Girls' and boys' facilities are identical but delineated by large-scale floor-to-ceiling graphics, depicting easily readable images of male, female and disabled forms.

Feilden + Mawson carried out research by talking to children aged between five and 18, equipping some with digital cameras to record what they most liked and disliked about

their immediate environment. Without exception toilets were described as the most hated element. For children, toilets are an emotive issue transferring into physical form their insecurities about school, privacy and bodily functions. Adults often patronize children by thinking what they want are small-scale stalls and low toilets when in fact this is alienating and not what they are used to at home. Consultation revealed that infants and teenagers alike desired spacious and intimate areas with mirrors for grooming, which was surprising as this aspect of daily routine was also ridiculed by them.

The design, which resulted from the investigations is both adult and sophisticated, with the toilets being the type normally found in a television studio or nightclub. A large part of the budget for the area was spent on Philippe Starck sanitaryware. Using such cutting-edge basins was found to encourage children to wash their hands. The colour scheme is in the same intense blue as all the core functions of the project, which was a directional ploy to orientate people with varying abilities and special needs. Lighting is ambient and fixtures and finishes are simple and unfussy.

'The children and young people using the OCC do regularly comment on the restrooms in a positive way; they are a talking point, their users have been flattered by the design which is, of course, a good thing,' says Josephine Harkins at Feilden + Mawson.

top
Easily readable graphics announce the male, female and disabled facilities.

opposite
The use of bold colours, soft curves and warm lighting makes the interiors of the OCC look bright and cheerful. The atmosphere is inviting and encourages interaction, allowing children to open up and talk about their problems.

right
Stalls are spacious and contain a mirror for private grooming. All doors are 1 metre (about 3 feet) wide, making the space accessible for the disabled or carers with young children. Cisterns are hidden with flow-flush sensors.

opposite
The sanitaryware is of a cutting-edge design. Philippe Starck basins are an exciting curiosity for the children and make them want to wash their hands after using the toilet.

Maag Recycling Factory
OOS
Winterthur, Switzerland

The concrete block of the recycling plant is made less forbidding for the local community by the insertion of a glass wall through which the corporate green of Maag Recycling advertises the company's ecological forward-thinking.

Corporate green has been used throughout the space. The shower room is dominated by the communal circular wash fountain. The pump is activated by means of foot pedals which permit water to flow only when depressed.

Switzerland has long been known for its ecological responsibility; recycling is as much a part of daily family life as a trip to the shops.

Maag Recycling organizes the collection of industrial and post-consumer goods and materials, such as glass, plastics, paper and metals, and has been located in a factory next to the main road and railway lines into Winterthur for more than 60 years. Following a period of expansion, the company wanted to cover over an outside yard to increase the footprint and therefore the productivity of their plant. However, Zurich-based architects oos had other ideas in mind when they built their factory in 2004 and restrooms in 2006. Considering Maag's location on the edge of a residential area, they developed a concept for a hybrid, multi-functional space that would improve the recycling process by allowing locals to deliver their waste directly to the factory. At the same time, their design allowed the town's workers and residents to enjoy the benefits of a public garden, rentable rooftop parking and outside terrace.

On the southern side of the site individuals deliver used products, moving their waste in specially designed carts from car to container; each is clearly labelled by hanging signage made from the material to be recycled. To the north of the warehouse, commercial trucks unload industrial waste ready to be sorted according to type and destination. The concrete block's industrial aesthetic is mitigated by the use of the company's corporate colour, a strong primary green, and a translucent glass wall which looks towards the residential neighbourhood.

The restrooms illustrated here are for the benefit of the largely male workforce (female and office/visitors restrooms did not fall under the brief of oos). The concept was to enlarge and reorganize the existing area to provide an environment in which the staff could change and wash, store their belongings and spend their breaks. Taking as their starting point the corporate ideology of Maag (economical use of natural resources, cost efficiency and simple functionality), oos have created a straightforward yet inviting interior to contrast with the rough industrial character of the surrounding plant. Fixtures, fittings and finishes were selected to be durable, user-friendly and understated so that no one detail dominates, allowing the use of corporate green to become the main feature. The glaring coloured surfaces are enhanced by a simple repetitive pattern of lights, circular in form, which mimic the two large dome skylights that allow natural light into the space. Following the ecological theme of the building, the client asked for low energy and water consumption. The urinals are waterless and do not need any electrical connections or water supplies and the toilets have a two-button flush system. The circular wash fountain is equipped with pneumatic foot pedals, which permit the water to run only when activated. All lights are attached to motion detectors and glow when someone is present in the room; otherwise the space remains naturally lit.

While many recycling plants are often hidden on vast industrial estates in out-of-town locations, this forward-thinking plant brings recycling to the people. Alternating between public and private functions and combining open with closed spaces, Maag has forged links among the local community, the environment and the needs of its commercial, municipal and individual clients.

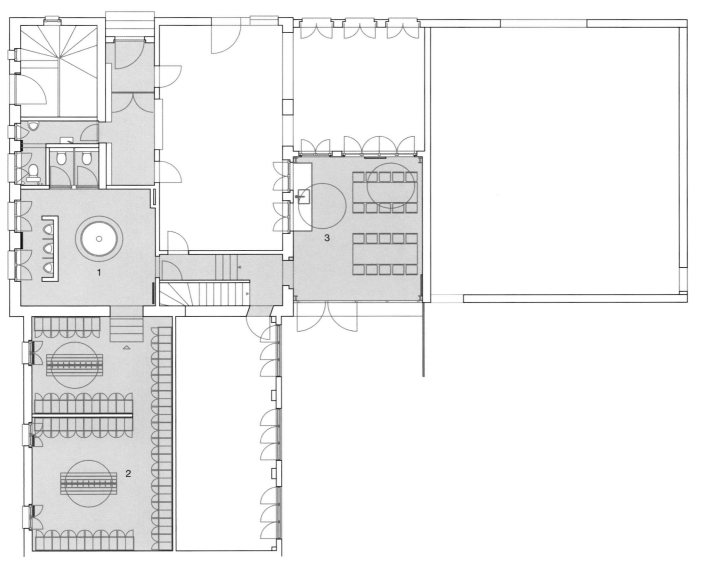

left
Floor plan showing the location of the toilets, washing facilities, changing area and common room in relation to one another. The facilities are situated in the office block, which was completed in 2006, two years after the plant. 1 Washroom/restrooms 2 Lockers and changing room 3 Kitchen/employee breakroom

opposite left and middle
The fixtures and fittings were selected to be functional and unobtrusive, and are all fitted with the latest water and energy-saving technology.

opposite right
The locker room is the centre of the restroom complex, adjacent to which the toilets and the shower room are located.

Dr Finklestein's Orthopaedic Practice
Mateja Mikulandra-Mackat
Berlin, Germany

Mateja Mikulandra-Mackat's design for Dr Matthias Finklestein's holistic treatment centre is as far away as one can get from the clinical white spaces which are prevalent in the design for this kind of medical environment.

Taking the concept of orthopaedics as her starting point, she has researched the human locomotive system and applied the result to a series of rooms dedicated to the examination and treatment of patients suffering from various degrees of skeletal malfunction. Dr Finklestein uses both conventional and alternative methods on his patients and his brief was to reflect this pluralistic attitude in the interiors of the surgery.

The architecture of the rooms is full of references to movement and posture; the former in horizontal accents and the latter in vertical motifs. The established and more unconventional medical practices are referenced by the use of both high- tech and low-tech elements, as well as contemporary and traditional detailing. Lighting has been skilfully employed throughout to articulate the spaces that are most significant in terms of communication and interaction, such as the reception and hallway.

Two features strike the client when first entering the surgery: the use of both graphics and colour. The reception desk and adjacent wall are emblazoned with enlarged black-and-white prints of the naked male form. The figure, in a squatting position, alludes to the suppleness and agility which are sought by Dr Finklestein's patients. These signifiers have been used as a leitmotif by the architect, with the desk and overhead canopy to the waiting room area given a serpentine, spine-like curvature to enforce connotations of the healthy human body.

The use of colour throughout has been based on *Mensche, Farbe, Raum*

left
The reception area is dominated by a curved reception desk emblazoned with black-and-white images of the naked male form; a motif which extends to the adjacent wall and door to the patient restroom, and alludes to the suppleness and agility sought by Dr Finklestein's patients.

opposite
The patient's restroom has unrestricted floor space to aid those with impaired mobility. The vanity area and toilet are separated by a translucent glass screen.

('Man, Colour, Space') by Rodeck, Meerwein and Mahnke, a book which examines the effects of colour and light on human psychology. The largest areas, including the reception, waiting and treatment rooms, have been decorated in tones of peach and orange, which according to colour theory produce a calming atmosphere, whereas brown laminate has been used on one wall to create an 'enveloping' ambience.

What is most striking about the unisex restrooms, one for the patients and one for the staff, is that they are finished in a complementary colour scheme to the rest of the interiors. The warm tones have been replaced by relaxing blues and whites; the walls clad in Bisazza 'Opus Romano' tiles. The demarcation was intentional. The restrooms offer a moment of repose: for the patients a time to stand back from their often exacting treatments and for the staff a chance to relax during their hectic working day. Mosaic was selected to create a 'dissolving' atmosphere, a digital picture

in which all tensions and problems break down to more manageable constituents. The fixtures and fittings were installed to create a feeling of luxury. A floating oak vanity unit is anchored along a side wall and the Philippe Starck toilets are hidden behind a translucent etched glass door.

In the restrooms, all reference to the body as machine has been replaced in favour of the body as a temple to be taken care of and pampered. These semi-private spaces serve to exemplify Dr Finklestein's holistic approach to his patients. Cool, static and soothing, they create a moment of tranquillity within the overall dynamic, colourful interiors of the rest of the surgery.

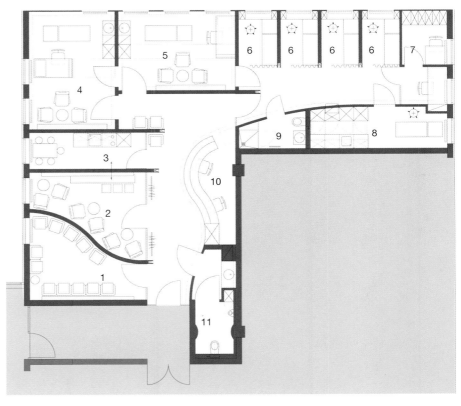

Dental Clinic KU64
Graft
Berlin, Germany

bottom
The lounge creates a new typology for a dental waiting room. No longer a space of fear and anticipation, it has been turned into a dune landscape with integrated seats and soft benches.

opposite
The main feature in the restrooms is the communal wash and dental care area. Here, glass sinks float in a water filled basin, casting patterns of light on to the ceiling. A glass panel over which water continually cascades fills the space with the sound of freshness.

Since the Hotel Q in fashionable west Berlin hit the design media in 2005, Graft, the international design firm with offices in Los Angeles, Berlin and Beijing, has quickly built up a reputation for being one of the most exciting and innovative practices around. The partners, Wolfram Putz, Thomas Willemeit and Lars Krückeberg, conceive interiors not as a series of static architectural spaces but as narratives – a cinematographic storyboard that helps the team to define a new way of thinking.

The concept for Dr Ziegler's KU64 dental clinic is a radical departure from the sterile, intimidating aesthetic usually associated with visiting the dentist. Graft asked itself the following questions:

'Why should a dental clinic engender a feeling of physical and psychic state of emergency and even abuse? Why instead shouldn't it promote connotations of beauty, health and wellbeing?'

The result of their deliberation is a dune landscape of undulating folded floors, rising to form the walls and reflected by a ceiling of a similar shape. The space is configured to allow privacy and intimacy, as well as openness and wide views, and constantly changes as it is traversed. Furniture and technical equipment are hidden in storage spaces within the sculpture of the building.

The treatment rooms are situated on either side of the lounge. Dental waiting rooms are notorious for being areas of fear and anticipation, with little to distract the patient from the clinical smells of the surgery and the sounds of the drills. In KU64, this has been translated into a welcoming large space with an adjacent outside sun deck; a beach scenario with integrated seats and soft benches, grouped around a free-hanging fireplace. A wireless local area network is provided for those who want to work, and 'sand castles' with video and gaming possibilities entertain the children. The reception doubles as a coffee shop and the olfactory sensation of burning wood and freshly ground coffee promote feelings of leisure and containment.

Walking from the dunes, down to the sea, the unisex restroom, or 'mouth spa', as Graft calls it, provides a very different experience. The restrooms are unremarkable in design but offer private refuges behind the main feature of the space, which is the communal wash and dental care area. In contrast to the lounge, while still complementing the whole theme of the clinic as a space of relaxation, clear geometry, indirect lighting and water features play with the

notion of purity. Instead of the sterile white appearance of most dental clinics, KU64's interiors are both organic and artistic. There is a water basin with floating glass sinks, reflecting light onto the ceiling, and a glass panel over which water cascades fills the space with the sound of freshness, evoking what Graft refers to as a 'futuristic image of a grotto with its own rituals'.

As dental care changes to offer not only the routine check-up but also services such as preventative consultation and cosmetic treatments, KU64 creates a new typology to reflect this departure. It offers an environment in which patients can forget their fears and relax in a way that they would usually expect from a spa, a café or a hotel.

CCA Graduate Center prefabricated restrooms
Jensen & Macy Architects
San Francisco, USA

Jensen & Macy have built up an international reputation for their poetic responses to a project's possible constraints.

To accommodate the expansion of the California College of the Arts, they were faced with the conundrum of squeezing 32 individual work studios for the graduate fine art students into a dilapidated 930 square metre (10,000 square foot) warehouse across the road from the main college. The work had to be carried out within three months, on a low budget. To add to the problem, the building was on a short ten-year lease and it needed to be improved seismically, heated and made accessible for all, including the disabled. In addition, its industrial heritage had resulted in a space without natural light, which was inconvenient for art students.

The solution was to strip the original structure back to its shell and start again. The exterior was clad in corrugated cement board and surmounted by a continuous clerestory of twin wall polycarbonate – a translucent material which allowed diffuse natural light to flood the interiors. Maintaining the industrial aesthetic, concrete flooring, exposed ducting and steel seismic cross-bracing inform the interior, while 3 x 3.7 metre (10 x 12 foot) individual plywood-clad studios rise no higher than the clerestory to maximize the light. Hallways ring the studios, widening at each end to form exhibition spaces.

To make the most of the space, the restroom was placed outside the building in an exterior courtyard. Adhering to the principle of pre-fabrication used elsewhere in the project, Jensen & Macy collaborated with the plumbing and sanitaryware manufacturer Kohler in the conversion of a mobile shipping

container. The unit was fitted out with fixtures, lighting, heating and finished in the factory, transported across country by truck, lifted into place with a crane and 'plugged in' to the utility connections on site. Students are notorious for the wear and tear that they put on any building and the elegantly utilitarian toilets, male and female occupying different sides of the restroom unit, were designed to be durable and easy to maintain. All the sanitaryware is fixed with low-flow water conservation mechanisms.

Visible from the road, the black metal box container has become a graphic sign for the school. The overall design for the extension of the CCA was awarded an AIA San Francisco Design Award; the jury particularly admired 'the witty pre-fabricated restrooms as well as the celebration of prosaic low-cost materials – all richly sublimated by careful juxtapositioning and detailing'.

left
The interiors are elegant but utilitarian. All fixtures are by the plumbing and sanitaryware manufacturer Kohler who collaborated on the container's fit-out.

opposite top left
The metal shipping container was craned into place and plugged into the utilities on site.

opposite bottom left
The unit contains male and female restrooms and is easily accessible by the disabled.

opposite right
The Graduate Center of the CCA was housed in a former dark and dilapidated warehouse. The architects stripped the original building back to its studs, cladding the walls in concrete and adding a polycarbonate clerestory that allowed light to flood into the interiors. Individual plywood studios suggest the minimal look of the work of Donald Judd.

Public Venues

Geberit Headquarters
designrichtung
Jona, Switzerland

Geberit Vertriebs is the leading Swiss manufacturer of innovative, durable and eco-friendly sanitaryware. In 2005, designrichtung was given the commission to refurbish the entrance hall, reception and first floor of their headquarters as part of a scheme to bring the offices, originally designed in the early 1960s, into the twenty-first century.

Jérôme Gessaga and Christof Hindermann's work at designrichtung lays strong emphasis on the importance of the human element in design. They had originally been commissioned by Geberit in 2003 to create an exhibition area for internal training purposes within the manufacturer's new information centre. The concept was to explore the topic of 'public and semi-public conveniences'. Passing through three zones, visitors were shown the importance of creating a positive atmosphere by using simple methods: light, materials, smells and colour, all of which affect the mood of people using restrooms.

The brief for the new façade and interiors of the headquarters was to form an architectural link with the training centre located opposite, and to relate exterior with interior. Employees are

bottom left
A sparkling curtain made from suspended cistern chains arouses the interest of those waiting in the foyer.

bottom right
The ground floor is given a spacious feel through the use of a muted colour scheme, high ceilings and reflective floor. The anteroom to the toilets is decorated in monochromatic red, which adds an element of surprise to the overall scheme.

opposite top
The ceiling of the anteroom is low which gives the impression of a narrow space and emphasizes the higher ceilings of the toilet area beyond.

opposite bottom
Ground floor plan showing the toilets located adjacent to the conference rooms towards the rear of the building. 1 Waiting area 2 Reception desk 3 Chain curtain 4 Reception 5 Anteroom 6 Meeting rooms 7 Female restroom 8 Male restroom 9 Lift to offices

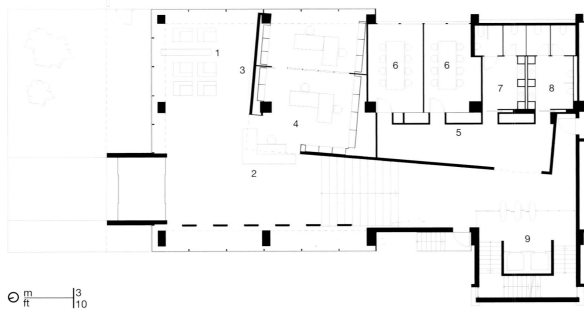

○ m ─── |3
  ft |10

drawn towards the interior through a new forecourt on the north side of the building. The entrance, reception and ground floor are given a sense of space without being overwhelming, with an emphasis placed on comfort and welcome. Visual accents, such as the Geberit logo on a sparkling curtain made from suspended cistern chains, arouse the interest of those waiting in the foyer.

The concept for the male and female restrooms, situated to the rear of the ground floor, was to demonstrate the emotive side of innovative technology. The anteroom is designed as a low-ceilinged space to emphasize the height of the toilet area. Cherry red is used to create an ambience which is both inviting and inspiring. Once inside the toilet and washroom space, the resin walls are decorated with brightly coloured tropical rainforest scenes, designed by Simon Burkhardt, who selected flora for the female and fauna for the male restrooms.

The graphics and pink reflector lamps, custom-made by designrichtung, are multiplied to infinity in the large mirrored niches. An amusing detail is the incorporation of a fly in the jungle graphics near the male cubicles which ironically refers to the images of insects traditionally placed in urinals to assist aim.

For Gessaga & Hindermann, toilets play a central role in any interior as they offer a possibility for retreat; a short moment to switch off and relax. There is no other room in which the interaction between space and well-being is so strongly linked. Often ignored as an area in which a designer can be creative, a small unconventional idea can provoke a lot of attention. designrichtung's concept for Geberit balances function with surprise in a space which underlines their philosophy: 'Through ordinary, everyday phenomena, we would like to see human curiosity play a more important part in our everyday lives again.'

top
designrichtung's 2003 exhibition design for Geberit's information centre. Divided into three zones, they create impact through colour, lighting and materials. The toilet area uses innovative technology, visuals and materials.

opposite
Rejecting the notion that a sterile white aesthetic equates to cleanliness, tropical rainforest graphics were used in the headquarter restrooms to enliven the space. These are reflected into infinity in the mirrored niches surrounding the washbasins in the female restroom. The lights were custom-made by designrichtung.

03
Hotels

Hotel Puerta América
Various
Madrid, Spain

The Hotel Puerta América is unique. A cornucopia of superstar architecture takes the visitor on an exploratory journey through a variety of different atmospheres. With each of the 12 floors designed by one of the world's leading architects or designers, it is possible to spend every night for nearly two weeks in a dozen distinctive environments. Add to this the reception, restaurant, bar, rooftop spa and subterranean garage, each again conceived by a different hand, and the result is a fascinating showcase of personal concepts of space. Unusual for a building of such a size, the client Hotel Silken imposed few creative or budget restrictions. This allowed the architects and designers involved to be as experimental as they wished. The individuals were selected for their expertise in various disciplines. Among them were John Pawson and Christian Liagre (interior designers); Sir Norman Foster, Zaha Hadid, Arata Isozaki and Jean Nouvel (architects); Ron Arad and Marc Newson (product designers); Javier Mariscal (graphic designer); and Victorio Lucchino (fashion designer). Each worked in total isolation from one another, creating 16 entirely separate projects within one building.

The bathrooms designed for the individual floors illustrate the wide variety of styles, surfaces and ambiences created by the various architects. On the seventh floor, Arad has used an industrial modular concept in LED Hi-Mac material with toilet, bath and shower integrated into one unit. Hadid has produced her first-floor design in her signature, digitally inspired, fluid and sinuous lines, again in expensive Hi-Mac. Plasma, the young UK-based team who won a competition to work on the hotel, are becoming known for their geometric lines and difficult shapes, seen here in the glossy, angular bathroom on the fourth floor, whereas Foster's second floor concept is an essay in elegant high-tech.

The reception and public restrooms were designed by John Pawson in his inimitable minimalist style. His aim was to create 'a zone of peace at the very heart of the hotel'. The toilet area replicates the concept of the reception. Shuttered with sandblasted glass from the hotel's foyer, a commotion of flushing sounds is set off as guests enter the space, triggering lights and water to rush down travertine walls opposite the washbasins. By using a pale ash wood for the walls and floor, natural stone for the sink, and carving the space with light, Pawson has created an interior from a limited range of materials that is austere yet luxurious. The panels on the stall doors echo the semicircle partition in the reception, which divides this area and the lifts from the quiet retreat where guests can sit and read the newspaper.

Nouvel, who designed the façade, rooftop spa and twelfth-floor suites, reflects positively on the fragmented design of the hotel: 'Of course it's not a symphony, it's a lot of little songs. It's a museum of one night … it's a very light exercise but it's a great experience.'

left and opposite
**Views into a selection
of bathrooms on
individual floors
illustrate the variety
of styles, surfaces
and atmospheres
designed by the
various architects:
Ron Arad has used
an industrial modular
concept on the
seventh floor (top
left); Zaha Hadid
has produced her
signature, digitally
inspired, fluid lines
on the first floor
(bottom left to
centre); Sir Norman
Foster's concept on
the second floor is
an elegant high-tech
essay (bottom right);
and Plasma's design
on the fourth floor is
glossy and angular
(opposite).**

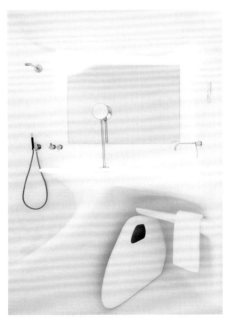

Blue Heaven Radisson SAS Hotel
Ground floor by Tihany Design
Frankfurt, Germany

Adam D. Tihany is considered the pre-eminent hospitality designer in the United States, with a string of famous restaurants and hotels to his name including the Bice and Spago restaurants worldwide, the Aleph Hotel in Rome, the Mandarin Bar at the Mandarin Oriental Hyde Park in London and the Dan Eilat Hotel and Resort in Israel. Using luxurious materials, fittings and furnishings in a contemporary and sensual way, all his interiors share a sense of exuberance and surprise.

There were three architects who worked on Blue Heaven, the new Radisson SAS Hotel in Frankfurt: John Seifert, the building architect; Matteo Thun, who created the guestrooms; and Adam D. Tihany, who designed the hotel lobby, library, lounge, bars, all-day dining room and brasserie.

left
The lobby is characterized by its openness and fluidity. The main focus is the glass staircase, which rises to a suspended wine bar and to the conference rooms. Its balustrades are etched with a rainbow-patterned relief, which plays on the themes of transparency and reflection.

bottom left
The partitions of stalls are clad in plastic, laminated with digital printed photos. The doors to the stalls have no frames or metal hinges, allowing the photograph to extend across the space without interruption.

opposite
The naked female silhouettes are explicit yet subtle as they peer seductively from behind the stalls in male toilets or dance past urinals.

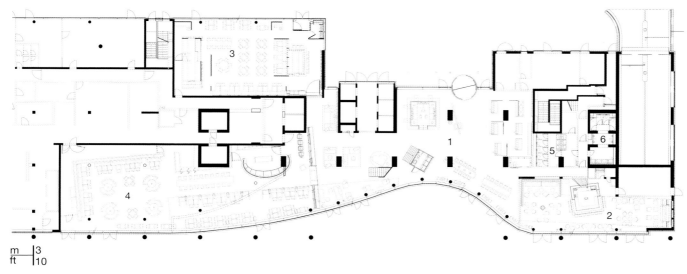

The overall concept for the hotel is centred around transparency. The interiors are spacious and loft-like, and defined by architectural features and furnishings rather than dividing walls. The free layout and the use of concrete, glass and steel lend the public spaces a luxurious yet industrial atmosphere, a direct reference to the city's intellectual and financial aspects. Tihany is a great advocate of site-specific architecture, and insists that 'the customer should be able to feel the rhythm of the city'.

The lobby is characterized by a translucent glass stairway, which joins the ground floor to a suspended wine room, and to the conference rooms above. A vibrant rainbow has been laminated into the balustrades, allowing a significant portion of clear glass to remain transparent while playing with cast shadow and reflection. 'The light coming through the rainbow balustrade creates quite a magical experience ... the colourful ambience adds to the feeling of luxury and uniqueness we wanted to create for the privileged hotel guests in Blue Heaven,' says Tihany.

The restrooms serve the ground floor facilities and continue the themes found in the rest of the interiors: comfort, distinctiveness, transparency, reflection and shadow play. However, whereas the reception and entrance hall have an almost engineered aesthetic, the private areas are much warmer and more personal. Tihany has used the opportunity to be playful and creative.

The separate male and female restrooms were designed to complement one another and are delineated by the use of gender-specific graphics and the colour of the glass sinks: yellow for the ladies and blue for the men. The flooring adheres to the same motif as the adjacent areas but is finished in dark grey Tijuca stone, while the walls are covered in a modern and contemporary trapezoidal pattern of earthy coloured local stones. The main feature of the design, however, is the sexy use of graphics. Silhouetted, naked women spy out of the cubicles and dance along the walls behind the urinals in the male restrooms, while a well-formed, muscular torso hugs the plastic laminated doors of

the female cubicles, which were custom-made without frames or metal hinges to allow the image to extend across the surface without interruption. Tihany wanted a strong decorative element, which would tantalize but be tasteful. Unlike the toilets at the Sofitel Hotel in Queenstown (see page 92) these images will not cause performance anxiety but subtly and stylishly allude to the intimate nature of these semi-private and public spaces.

top
Floor plan of the ground floor, showing the male and female restrooms situated to the right of the lobby.
1 **Lobby** 2 **Cigar bar**
3 **Brasserie**
4 **Restaurant**
5 **Female restrooms**
6 **Male restrooms**

opposite
The female and male restrooms have the same essential elements but are delineated by the colours of the sinks, and gender-specific graphics. The female restroom has a single digital photographic image of a naked male torso running the length of the stalls. A free-standing opaque yellow glass sink is made to glow by the use of artfully placed floor lights.

Sofitel
Perron
Photography by Sheena Haywood
Queenstown, New Zealand

Using subtle lighting, expensive materials and sanitaryware, the male restrooms at Queenstown's new Sofitel hotel are tastefully executed. The restrooms, however, while perhaps not as cutting-edge in terms of design, are certainly notable for the amount of publicity they generated both nationally and abroad for their more titillating graphics. They are such a talking point locally that men are queuing for the privilege of unzipping their trousers in front of life-size photographs of a selection of the area's most beautiful models.

The hotel, built in 2006, is comfortable, but unremarkable in its architecture and design. So, the developers Perron wanted to create something a little special for the second-floor male urinals, which serve the restaurants and shopping areas in the hotel's complex. The original idea was to include a large feature window wall behind the urinals depicting distinctive imagery of Queenstown. This concept developed into including figures in the landscape so the user could imagine himself as part of the action, standing on the edge of a bungee jump or on the top of a mountain. After several

attempts, the concept wasn't working so stock photography was used to come up with new proposals, one of which included an audience at the opera looking and applauding. Yet the developer was still not satisfied and wanted a more 'edgy' look, so commissioned a shoot by Queenstown photographer Sheena Haywood to add sex appeal to the voyeuristic theme. Haywood took images of a series of models, all dressed in provocative clothing with shocked expressions and instruments of measurement or appraisal in their hands. 'We had a lot of fun with the shoot, made

IT'S NOT THE SIZE OF THE INSTRUMENT THAT COUNTS

SOFITEL IS PROUD TO SPONSOR THE

ASB JAZZFEST QUEENSTOWN 14th - 23rd OCTOBER 2006

The male restroom on the second floor of Sofitel's hotel and shopping centre features a 6 metre (20 feet) photographic mural placed behind the urinals. Six local models have full view of the action and their faces tell the story.

It is Sofitel's intention to change the graphics on a frequent basis. The urinal graphics were changed for the Queenstown Jazz Festival, sponsored by the hotel chain.

all the better for the fact that there weren't any men there when we did it,' she says.

The life-size graphics were placed so they could stand in judgement on the size, or lack of it, of the men's credentials as they lined up to relieve themselves: one woman holds a pair of binoculars while another has a tape measure in her hand; one is taking pictures, a second raises her glasses in disbelief while a third slowly starts to undress herself. Whether this has resulted in performance anxiety is hard to say, although it's well known that men find it difficult to relieve themselves in front of an audience. One gentleman has been quoted as saying that 'Mona Lisa' eyes following his every move have the effect of cutting him off mid-flow.

Perron may be taking a light-hearted approach, but this is not the first time that such gimmicks have been employed in the bathroom. Esther Derkx's 'Kisses!' urinal, made of two luscious red lips crying out to be used, sold worldwide. Graphics, such as flies and bullseyes, encourage aim in commonplace settings, and two-way mirrored cubicles can often be seen in restrooms in trendy nightclubs.

So New Zealand not only has great scenery and great sheep, but a reputation for the kinkiest urinals. If you want a tip, the curvy blond measuring a length is the most popular. Sofitel is now looking at decorating the female restrooms with something 'equally eye-catching'.

Hotel Duomo
Ron Arad Associates
Rimini, Italy

The entrance to the hotel is through pinball flipper-like doors, which frame the reception desk to create the focal point of the hotel.

left
The bronze of the façade meanders its way into the bar. The bar itself is an island with sinuous cut-outs. The top is bronze and the sides are made of polished stainless steel, their shiny surfaces creating distorted reflections.

opposite
Instead of being rooms with baths, the guestrooms are bathrooms with attached beds – they are Corian wetrooms forming backdrops to the sleeping areas.

The Hotel Duomo is tucked into the backstreets of Rimini, one of Italy's most famous seaside resorts. Since the 1960s Rimini has attracted tourists from around the world. What is less known is that this resort is also a highly creative university town frequented by fashion and design types, many of whom come here for business. It's this market which Pierpaolo Bernardi, the owner of the Duomo, wanted to target, when he set up the hotel.

The hotel is situated in a narrow street typical for this area of Emilia-Romagna. A hostelry had existed on the site since the 1950s but it was an outdated, rather shabby affair. Ron Arad clad the existing façade in a sheet of bronze which meanders into the building to form the back wall of the bar and terminates in the profile of a bench seat. The bar itself is

a large island, its bronze top articulated by curves and niches which form private drinking and dining areas. The sides are made of polished stainless steel, as are the irregularly placed supporting columns; the shiny surfaces create distorted 'magic mushroom' reflections of the hip crowds eating, drinking and listening to DJs flown in from New York, Milan and Ibiza.

The tour de force of the whole project is the reception desk, which dominates the foyer. Like a spinning coin which has not yet come to rest, the stainless-steel ring dramatically leans at an angle supported by a single polished steel column. The guest rooms are no less unique. Instead of being rooms with baths, they are bathrooms with attached beds – Corian wetrooms forming backdrops to the sleeping areas.

The silvery public restroom is located in the basement and complements the bronze ground-floor bar that it serves.

It is reached by way of a stairway, which is sandwiched between two full-height, polished stainless-steel mirrored walls. The shimmering descent sets the scene for the diurnal area below. With a black resin floor, and matt black walls and ceilings, the basement enhances the restroom, which was designed as a glass light box. The unisex restroom has two entrances and four cubicles. It is quite common in Italy for bars and restaurants to have one small restroom for both men and women but this normally takes the form of a single room with toilet and sink included. Arad's concept was to expand on the idea. The main wall is glass, allowing views from the corridor into the restroom's communal wash area. Behind the glass wall is a single, large, full-length stainless-steel sink with four Boffi taps. In front of each tap is a double-sided circular mirror – a sandwich of glass layers.

Customers can either check their appearance without going into the restrooms or have a degree of privacy to wash after using the toilets. All of the restroom's walls are either mirrored or have illuminated glass panels, giving rise to astonishing infinity reflections.

Arad was responsible for everything in the Hotel Duomo from the architecture right down to the fittings, furnishings and graphics. Known for his organic forms, experimentation with materials, exaggerated structural forms and large explosions of scale, Arad has created a destination hotel. There are more than 1,000 places in which to stay at Rimini but only one where you can do so with such theatricality.

far left
View looking from the bathrooms towards the corridor. The stainless-steel sink stretches the full length of the glass wall, catching reflections of light.

left
All the restroom's walls are mirrored or have illuminated glass panels, giving rise to astonishing infinity reflections.

opposite top
The main wall of the restroom is glass with circular double-sided mirrors set above each sink. Patrons can use the mirrors from the corridor without entering the restroom space.

opposite bottom left
Floor plan of the basement showing the location of the unisex restroom which serves the bar area above.
1 Unisex restroom

opposite bottom right
The basement is totally black with resin floor and matt walls, enhancing the shimmering, jewel-like quality of the restrooms.

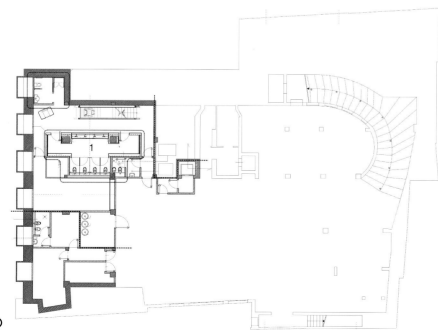

Lloyd Hotel
MVRDV in collaboration with
Christian Seyforth and Atelier Van Lieshout
Amsterdam, The Netherlands

bottom left
Pre-fabricated toilet units arrive in front of the monumental and imposing façade of the Lloyd Hotel, built in 1921 by architect Evert Breman.

bottom right
The Snel (fast) restaurant is the main focus of the hotel and is located in MVRDV's bright and open central atrium, which also houses the Cultural Embassy in a series of suspended boxes and platforms.

opposite
The communal bathroom serves the two-star rooms which are without ensuite facilities. Apart from a minor restoration of the institutional cream tiles and the provision of modern fittings, the interior remains much the same as when it was built in the 1920s.

Commissioned by the Dutch shipping company the Koninklijke Hollandsche Lloyd, the Lloyd Hotel was built in 1921 to house Eastern European emigrants bound for the New World. During the Second World War, the Nazis took over the hotel and used it as a detention centre. Following the German occupation the hotel remained a prison until 1963, when it became a young offenders' institution and finally, rundown and largely ignored, a squat for artists.

The Lloyd is situated in the former eastern dock district of Amsterdam, the Oostelijke Handelskade, and is central to the huge regeneration programme which the area has witnessed in recent years. The commission for its renovation was given to MVRDV in collaboration with Christian Seyforth and the interior designer/artist Joep Van Lieshout. Their brief was to pay homage to the chequered history of the building while creating a new venture in the hospitality industry. The hotel not only serves its guests but acts as a social hub for Amsterdammers, who can enjoy the 24-hour restaurant and bar, read a book in the design library, or participate in arts events via its Cultural Embassy.

Many of the internal spaces, as well as the monumental and foreboding façade, were listed. MVRDV integrated the preserved areas: the skin, old ticket office, wood panelling and tile work with

bright, open and contemporary spaces, including the majority of bedrooms, plus the central atrium that reaches up through six floors and houses the Snel (fast) restaurant and the Cultural Embassy.

The 120 guest rooms are unique and range from economy two-star to luxury five-star accommodation. The cheapest rooms are without bathrooms but are supplied with fluffy dressing gowns for the trip down the hall to the ascetic communal toilet and shower room which, apart from a scrub-up of its original institutional cream tiles and the addition of a few red geraniums, has not changed since the 1920s. At the other end of the spectrum, the more expensive rooms have specially designed bathrooms

by Atelier Van Lieshout (AVL), which make a feature from a hotel typology that is usually no more than a partition minimizing the room size. Different suites were given different concepts and the various sanitary units formed a major part of these. Produced from brightly coloured polyester, the sculptural interventions are recognizable as AVL's work. Made to measure, cantilevered boxes open to reveal baths and toilets, while in some cases, shower rooms can only be reached by ladder.

Famous for blurring the lines between art, architecture and design, the Lloyd's bathrooms are not the first time that AVL have designed modular restrooms. In 1999 they created a biomorphic form

housing the toilets for the café at the Boijmans Van Beuningen Museum in Rotterdam. In the Lloyd, the camouflaged unit of polyester-coated foam stands like a Dadaist sculpture, its bright green interior and open design inviting users to treat it as an art form, as well as a functional convenience.

Lloyd Hotel

The 120 guest rooms are all unique. AVL's modular bathrooms add to the concept of each interior. Most of the sanitary units are made of polyester (top), but for the soundproofed Music Room (opposite), a five-star suite with walls clad in plywood.

right
A biomorphic form housing the toilets for the café at the Boijmans Van Beuningen Museum in Rotterdam, designed in 1998 by AVL.

Club Privé at the Ballagio Hotel
Tihany Design
Las Vegas, USA

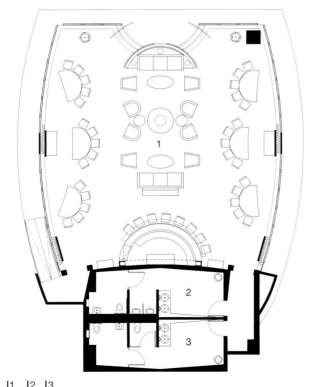

```
m |1  |2  |3
ft     |5   |10
```

The Club Privé is an exclusive gaming room and bar within the huge complex which is the Ballagio Hotel, one of the many mega-hotels and casinos that line the never-sleeping Strip of Las Vegas.

Adam D. Tihany was commissioned to work on this relatively small area and, as one of the world's leading hospitality designers, to add a touch of class to an environment dedicated to parting the high rollers from their fortunes.

A firm believer in site-specific architecture, Tihany seeks to convey a connection with the environment in which he is working and, as far as opulence goes, the Club Privé fits well into the rest of the interiors within the Ballagio. However, this elite private room was designed to be unique. An elevated floor enhances the exclusive nature of the space. The concept was to create a European feel with decorative accents to evoke the sumptuous Art Deco period. The ceiling and floor are finished with strong geometrical motifs that complement the rich metal, dark wood, glass and silver-leafed partitions in the gaming room. Polished chrome, mahogany, plush fabrics and calfskin upholstery in the bar and lounge contribute to a feeling of luxury and bring to mind the modernist ambience of the great ocean liners of the 1920s and 1930s. To counter-balance the solidity of the interiors, subtle lighting is achieved by Venetian glass panels and chandeliers.

The restrooms were designed to complement the lounge. Male and female areas are arranged next to one another in a symmetrical layout, with entrances side by side. The main feature of both zones is the polished stainless-steel sinks, which stand at right-angles to the mirrored wall. Reflections create a sculptural element resembling a gyroscope, with the fixtures and pipes adding to the composition. The sinks are separated from the marble counter-top by rings of stainless steel through which down-lighters cast haloes onto the floor. The shiny surfaces of steel and marble in turn reflect patterns onto the ceiling. The dynamic interplay of light and shadow produces a chiaroscuro effect animating the whole of the area. The walls are made of alternating textured and flat mahogany panels which add warmth to the machine-age interior and intensify the contrast of the lighting.

Tihany has worked many times in Las Vegas, a city which he considers to be 'unique – architecturally, demographically and culturally'. Dedicated to creating and delivering fantasy, and to entertaining, it is an ideal location for his luxurious and often themed extravaganzas. For Tihany, Las Vegas offers an opportunity to be experimental. With the many casinos, hotels and resorts all vying for customers there is a constant need for reinvention. Designers are given budgets where anything is possible, as design sells like nowhere else in the world.

right
The main feature of both restrooms is the sculptural sink element, which is created through a combination of structure, light and reflection, animated by shadows cast on both floor and ceiling.

opposite top
The concept behind the exclusive Club Privé evokes the sumptuous interiors of Art Deco lounges.

opposite bottom
Floor plan showing the location of the restrooms at the rear of the space. The male and female facilities are set side by side, creating a mirror image of one another. 1 Club Privé 2 Male restrooms 3 Female restrooms

Ono at the Gansevoort Hotel
Jeffrey Beers
New York, USA

Along with Adam D. Tihany and David Rockwell, Jeffrey Beers completes the triumvirate of American designers shaping the hospitality industry in the United States. He believes that the future of dining is entertainment. 'What I bring to restaurant concepts, to restaurateurs and spaces that I develop,' he explains, 'is a sense of theatre, or that the guest is in a dream. We're making movies here.'

Ono is located in the Gansevoort Hotel in the stylish Meatpacking District of Manhattan and is the latest of his collaborations with chef/entrepreneur Jeffrey Chodorow. Following the success of China Grill, Tuscan and Rum Jungle, the restaurant, bar and oriental covered dining terrace, which serves a fusion of traditional and contemporary Japanese cuisine, was much anticipated.

The concept of the design is based around the four elements – fire, water, earth and sky – which Beers developed into a multi-level venue offering a dining experience. It boasts an open kitchen, a fire-breathing robata grill, semi-private tatami booths, garden cabanas (one of which contains a Japanese soaking tub), wall-size paintings of yakuza body tattoos, a glass-bottom sushi bar and whimsical restrooms, which have been dubbed a 'technological' marvel.

At the front of house, sleek design and flattering lighting play vital roles in an interior that makes the clientele look as well as feel good. The loft-like main dining room is a vast space filled with deep red banquettes and glossy, ebony tables, lit by discreet pinpoint spots and overhead chandeliers designed to look like oriental paper lanterns. The three levels are connected by a grand staircase, which stands in front of back-lit walls lined with oversized sake bottles.

left
The main tri-level dining space is linked by a staircase which stands in front of back-lit walls lined with oversized sake bottles. The overall ambience of the interior is sultry and moody, reflected in the dark tones and warm furnishings.

right
The restrooms are dominated by a central, circular, communal wash area, lined with a brightly coloured mosaic, which is clearly visible from the main dining area. The male and female restrooms lead off the main space. The outstanding feature is the freestanding Corian and polished stainless-steel sink.

The restrooms were conceived as a diversion from the dark and moody restaurant, providing a surprise boost of colour and brightness. The area is dominated by a dramatically lit floating communal sink in Corian and polished stainless steel, with deep wood cabinetry surrounded by a circular, coloured mirror, and mosaic tiled wall. The central round space is a focal point, which is clearly visible from the main dining room and also serves to bring men and women together within intimate surroundings. The separate bathrooms are situated on either side of the communal space. They are brightly lit and finished with intense complementary colours selected especially for each of the sexes: red for the women and teal for the men. The stainless-steel finish and vibrant colours were selected to contrast with the restaurant's warm tones to achieve a yin/yang effect between the dining area and the restrooms. Lighting and reflection were key elements in heightening the experience. In the communal area, the circular mirrors reflect light to envelop the space in luminescence, while shining surfaces and wall-mounted mirrors make the small restrooms look bigger.

Unlike many architects who design their restrooms to complement the main concept of an interior, Beers has opted for a contrasting aesthetic, leading the user from one extreme to another through a communal area which is physically as well as visually linked to both areas. The whole experience adds to the restaurant's dramatic and sexy ambience.

bottom and opposite top
The male and female restrooms are bright and colourful spaces with stainless-steel walls and shiny doors and partitions. Red was selected for the women and teal for the men. The contrasting colours and finishes create a yin/yang effect, complementing the warm tones of the main dining area.

opposite bottom
The VIP restroom is situated on the second floor and contains the latest Toto toilet. While these fully automated space-age products, which wash, dry and play music, have been on the market for several years, they remain a talking point.

Mix at THEhotel
Patrick Jouin
Las Vegas, USA

Patrick Jouin is the creator of some of the most beautiful restaurants in the world, which combine poetry, mood and ambience in feminine and sensitive interiors. He describes himself as neither designer nor architect but a 'DJ of space', using light, experimentation with materials and technology to push the boundaries of what is possible.

The Mix restaurant is located on top of the Mandalay Resort Group's THEhotel with fantastic views over Las Vegas' famous Strip and the surrounding desert. The main dining area is reached through a dark, rust-coloured corridor, a theatrical device which intentionally lowers expectation, making the first glimpse of the restaurant all the more astonishing. The double-height, 12 square metre (130 square foot) white space is flooded with light and glimmers in an otherworldly fashion beneath a spectacular 8 metre (26 foot) chandelier – which is made from 15,000 hand-blown, transparent Murano glass 'bubbles' amid which a VIP lounge clad in silver leaf appears to float. Following Dante's footsteps into

the inferno, the fierce red lounge is as far away aesthetically as one can get from the celestial extravaganza of the restaurant. The space is dominated by the lacquered fibreglass island bar, which contains a private drinking area and shoots 'flames' and 'sparks' towards the ceiling.

As for the restrooms, Jouin was conscious of the fact that whatever he did in Mix would be competing with the view. In the restaurant and lounge he created dazzling spaces, but for the restrooms he used the world as his backdrop; the main feature of the area is Las Vegas itself. Situated at the end of the lounge, the stalls and urinals face floor-to-ceiling windows. The marble walls, ceiling, floor and sanitaryware are glossy black, which has the effect of making everything disappear, except the user who, reflected in the window, hovers over the lights of the city below. For Jouin, toilets are spaces in which architecture can create surprise. At Mix, the designer seems to have done very little; or rather he has done everything by dematerialising the concrete to heighten the ethereal. Who needs design when you have the stars.

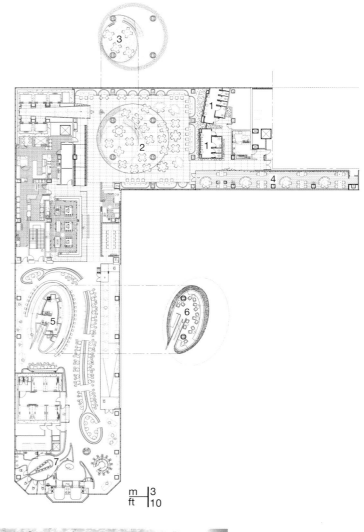

right
The toilets are shiny black boxes which dematerialize in front of floor-to-ceiling windows, leaving an ethereal portrait of the user suspended above the lights of Las Vegas below.

opposite top
Floor plan showing the two sets of restrooms. The ones which serve the 200-cover restaurant were simplified during the building process due to budget restrictions, and are not featured here. The lounge restrooms are located at the end of the 300-seat bar.
1 Restaurant restrooms 2 Restaurant 3 VIP lounge 4 Entrance corridor 5 Bar 6 Private drinking area 7 Lounge restrooms (as featured)

opposite bottom
The restaurant (right) and lounge (left) are visions of heaven and hell. Aesthetically opposed, they are both opulent spectacles intended to compete with the spectacular views of Las Vegas, afforded by the venue's rooftop location.

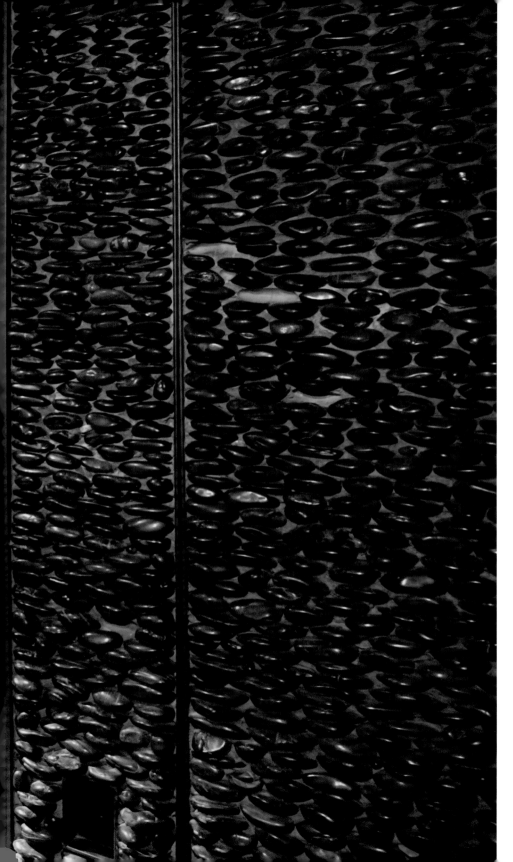

Bon Moscow
Philippe Starck
Moscow, Russia

Anything that world-famous designer Philippe Starck puts his name to is bound to be popular or at least create media attention. Bon Moscow is the third in his designs for the restaurant chain; The Parisian Bon and Bon Two are essays in refined elegance – more tasteful exercises than their exotic and macabre Russian counterpart.

Starck's latest Bon is certainly flamboyant – a baroque extravaganza that would not look out of place in the dining hall of Count Dracula's Transylvanian castle. Copulating couples dance in a frenzy of passion on frescoes artfully concealed by an eagle-headed throne, Baccarat candelabras ooze wax onto the tables, while black shaded lamps, adorned with the world's currency symbols, advertise the fact that you are certainly not there as the guests of the Billionaire Club which financed the operation. Starck's now infamous gold-plated Kalashnikov lights for Flos combine opulence with murder, a skull and crossbones underscored with a twirling band of razor wire decorates the shelves, stuffed owls drip jewellery and stained-glass windows – with images that would make William Blake eat his heart out – cast rainbow shades onto the diners below. Customers who take their

Restaurants

right and opposite right
The female restroom is brighter than the male facilities. However, the graffiti, with messages exhorting murder and revolt, picture how Empress Aleksandra's bathroom might have looked after she had been hauled away by the Bolsheviks.

opposite left
The baroque, extravagant restaurant interior, which glorifies a trinity of sex, violence and food.

I HATE

THE PEOPLE ARE THE HEROES

You got to be someone else.

left
The male restroom is
blackness incarnate.
Stained-glass
windows depicting
Christ on the Cross
are surrounded by
the most opulent of
baroque mirrors.

opposite
The dark interiors of
the male restrooms
are offset by luxuriant
stained-glass panels
bearing flaming
religious iconography.

places on a miscellany of mismatched chairs, some half-burned and treated with resin to preserve their gothic aesthetic, are lulled by a diurnal atmosphere. Eating from bespoke Limoges porcelain and drinking from the finest glass goblets, they are seduced by an interior which glorifies a trinity of sex, violence and food.

Whether an ironic take on Starck's declared dislike of a city, renowned for its gross excesses, a tongue-in-cheek comment on the 'rich man with no taste', or merely a creation of luxurious chaos as Starck would have you believe, the restaurant is an unqualified success, with not a table to be had for love nor money.

If having spent a fortune, you want to spend a penny, the restrooms continue the themes of *arriviste* grandeur. The male restrooms are black and foreboding, dominated by apocalyptic stained-glass back-lit panes with flaming religious imagery, while the female restrooms are decorated with fin-de-siècle gothic, which contrasts with the distressed plastered walls in murky shades of yellow and blue. Both use ornate mirrors, chandeliers and gold adornments, but alarmingly, each comes complete with its own designer graffiti exhorting the now affluent masses to murder and revolt.

Nobu Berkeley ST
David Collins Studio
London, UK

Nobu Berkeley ST marks the latest of international chef Nobuyuki Matsuhisa's chain of eponymous restaurants, serving a unique blend of Asian and Peruvian cuisine in venues from Hong Kong to Manhattan. The commission was given to the David Collins Studio, with a worldwide reputation for its amalgamation of the decorative and the architectural in sumptuous yet classic London restaurant interiors: Petrus, J. Sheekey, The Blue Bar and The Wolseley to name but a few.

The W1 location is expensive and exclusive yet Matsuhisa has chosen this elite setting (the site was the former home of the original Mayfair Club) to introduce a new and informal approach to dining, which eschews reservations in favour of a more democratic approach to the Nobu experience. David Collins's design complements this philosophy.

To reflect the commitment to fresh, natural ingredients and flavours in the restaurant, Collins has selected not to use an 'ethnic' aesthetic, but the enduring image of the tree as an underlying theme, combining this with elemental materials – wood, stone and metal – to form a series of spaces that, architecturally and conceptually, flow seamlessly together. In some areas, this theme is explicit, as where Collins himself has designed the sprawling tree light sculpture, whose branches reach out behind the bar. In the reception lobby, the artist Malcolm Hill has created an abstract forest mural, while in the restaurant the bright interior is complemented by a 10 metre (33 foot) arboreal tapestry. In other parts of the restaurant, a shimmering sylvan ambience has been suggested by soft plaster walls, fading from gold to silver and curving overhead to form a canopy of leaves, punctuated by trunk-like pillars clad in silky, smooth metal.

The male and female restrooms are situated besides the stairwell on the ground floor, which is the main circulation point between bar and restaurant. Unusually, more space has been given to the male restrooms but otherwise the spaces are identical. The area is designed with the same level of luxury as at the front of house, but as an antithesis to the calm contemporary mood of the restaurant. On entering, the user is confronted with a bold, almost violent,

left
The downstairs lounge has an arboreal theme. David Collins has designed the tree light sculpture, which dominates the bar. Shiny metal columns form trunks supporting the ceiling.

opposite
A bold and violent blood-red graphic layered with a mirror is the dominant feature in both the male and female restrooms.

right
Floor plan. Restrooms are situated next to the stairwell on the first floor. Unusually, more space has been dedicated to the male facilities. 1 Male restroom 2 Female restroom 3 Restroom lobby

opposite
The sinks are made from limestone, which ties them into the organic theme of the restaurant. The walls are hand-scratched Italian plaster.

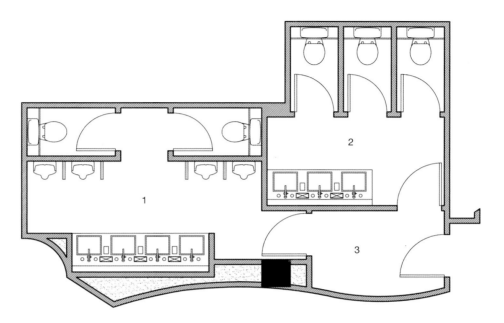

blood-red graphic, layered with a mirror which is enhanced by the surrounding dark and earthy colour palette. The surfaces are bold and strong, with walls in hand-scratched Italian plaster, and the floor in hard-wearing grey limestone. Collins believes it is important to make people feel both confident and attractive while using the restrooms. The well-constructed interiors have a solidity and permanence which give a protective atmosphere, while the lighting illuminates and enhances the main features of the design as well as the clientele. Functionality was Collins's starting point, with finishes chosen for their brightness and ease of maintenance. The fixtures and fittings continue Nobu's raw yet elegant aesthetic theme, with the sinks in limestone and the toilet pans and urinals selected for their curved profiles.

'My inspiration and brief from Nobu restaurants was to develop an organic, free-flowing design that incorporates all aspects of eating out, from bar and lounge to dinner and even late-night dancing,' says Collins. 'The restaurant is designed specifically for Nobu Berkeley ST and incorporates specially developed materials, finishes and artwork. It's Nobu for everybody.'

Morimoto
Tadao Ando
New York, USA

bottom
The main restaurant is dominated by a suspended textile ceiling hardened by fibreglass which alludes to the raked sands of a Japanese garden. The dining area and basement lounge are linked by a double-height wall made from 17,400 bottles, created by Ross Lovegrove for Ty Nant.

opposite
The client specified that all fittings should be white. The ambient lighting flatters the user and makes the polyurethane stall doors glow.

Morimoto is named after its chef, Masaharu Morimoto, and owned by award-winning restaurateur Stephen Starr, who already runs a Morimoto restaurant in Philadelphia. Starr has been credited with single-handedly putting Philadelphia on the gastronomic world map by commissioning internationally renowned designers (David Rockwell, Karim Rashid and India Mahdavi) to create 12 haute cuisine/design establishments over the last decade. Morimoto, and its sister restaurant Buddakan, are located next door to one another in the fashionable Meatpacking District in New York, and are Starr's first forays into world-class Manhattan dining.

Recognizing the importance of design in a competitive market, Starr wanted something completely different for his contemporary Japanese restaurant. So, he turned to Pritzker Prizewinner Tadao Ando, whose simple geometric forms, minimalist architecture and sensual use of concrete have garnered him international fame. Morimoto is Ando's first restaurant design and also his first project in New York. The design for the restaurant is not overtly Japanese but has a zen-like quality created by a subtle, monochromatic blending of materials, which adds warmth, texture and tactility to the interiors. Ando's signature use of unfinished concrete is modulated by an Isometrix lighting scheme, which enhances the serene ambience through a palette of concealed illumination. Surfaces are made to glow, adding levels of translucency that accent and soften the unforgiving material.

Ando believes that buildings are not just mechanical but should engender an emotive response. His architecture blends

the artificial with allusions to the natural. Morimoto is dominated by a rippling, suspended textile ceiling hardened by fibreglass, which recalls to the raked sands of a Japanese rock garden; and a 6 metre (20 foot) 'water wall', formed of 17,400 Ty Nant mineral water bottles (designed by Ross Lovegrove), containing warm and cold LEDs which give the effect of pools of sunlight on a pond. The transparent bar in the lounge, embedded with delicately veined leaves and Lovegrove's custom-designed furnishings continue the dialogue with the architecture, respecting its clear lines but adding a humanizing, organic quality.

The restrooms are more traditionally Japanese in style than any other part of the restaurant. Here water, concrete, light and nature blend in an aesthetic which combines the best of influences from traditional Japanese architecture with a unique modernist style.

Located in the basement adjacent to the lounge, male and female restrooms are situated either side of the corridor and, apart from the provision of urinals for the men, are the same in design. The chef demanded that all the fitments and finishes should be white and appliances hands-free with sensor-controlled taps and toilet seats which rise automatically as the user enters the cubicles. Hand-dryers are hidden beneath the bottom edge of the mirror over the sinks to emphasize the minimalist design of the space. Light is a controlling factor in all of Ando's works, and in the restrooms he has created an indirect and reflective ambient lighting, which illuminates the milky polyurethane stall doors, making them glow. On entering the cubicles, the magic truly begins. The back walls of each of these tiny spaces contain an infinity mirror filled with seasonal flowers: wisteria during the winter, plum in the spring, cherry-blossom for summer and Japanese maple in autumn. Like stepping through the wardrobe into the magical kingdom of Narnia, Ando has created an ethereal, contemplative world a million miles away from the bustle of the restaurant above and the siren-filled streets of Manhattan outside.

right
The toilets are state-of-the-art high-tech Japanese Toto appliances with a range of special features that can be adjusted to suit personal needs, including automatic toilet seat and flushing system, integral bottom cleaning water jets and deodorizer.

opposite
The small cubicles are made to look larger through the use of an infinity mirror, filled with seasonal flowers.

'P' Food and Wine
Simone Micheli
Turin, Italy

The 'P' Food and Wine restaurant and wine bar was completed in 2005 as a temporary architectural installation to introduce Piedmontese cuisine to an international clientele during the Olympic Winter Games held in Turin in 2006.

The interior of the restaurant (opposite) features soft, organic coloured surfaces and is animated by multi-media projections. It makes a contrast with the wine bar (right), which uses an industrial aesthetic of reflective glass, metal and laminates.

Emphasizing its transient function, the restaurant interiors have an ethereal ambience but are grounded by concrete architectural principles: colour, images, sound, light and taste combine with formal elements and a methodical application of various building materials, which marries the conceptual with the functional. The architect, Simone Micheli, who designed all aspects from the space itself, to the graphics, waiters' uniforms and place settings, describes it as a 'synergy celebrating the relationship between man, constructed space and food'.

Three walls of the main space are veiled in semi-transparent white organza curtains which move in the air currents, breaking down the stereotypical concept of a solid boxed space. Mixing soft and organic with hard and industrial, the fourth wall is finished in a shiny black laminate and the floors are formed from anodized aluminium slats. Oversized chrome adjustable lamps spotlight forms and details, while neon lights curve along the top of the curtains, infusing them with fuchsia luminescence. White wall lights placed at varying heights animate the surfaces by pulsating randomly. At selected moments all light dims, windows and doors are covered by electronic blinds, and projectors cast images of Piedmont onto the gauze which, still gently undulating, brings the landscape magically to life.

Further rooms, such as a gathering area, a sales point, a restaurant, a first-floor VIP area and terrace, also combine soft sculptural forms and furnishings with shiny, reflective laminate and metal surfaces; the interiors are animated by media projections, coloured lighting effects and the shadowy figures of the guests as they move around the space.

The unisex restroom creates a dialogue with the main spaces, at one moment complementing and the next contradicting elements within the overall concept of the restaurant and wine bar. Work was limited to the communal washroom as the pre-existing toilets had to be retained. Micheli conceived a sensory space where the users become protagonists within the design. Unlike the restaurant, the interior is hard and dark with strong accents of bright, white light silhouetting the photographic male and female figures outlined on the opaque, glass doors. The light is cast diffusely onto the shiny PVC floors and adhesive black plastic wrapped walls. The sink area lies below a mirror set within the black laminate wall opposite the door; the reflections double the restricted space. The only accents of colour are the blue neon words announcing the water, soap and drying cells, controlled by electronic sensors, contained within a rectangular steel aperture above the basins.

Micheli sees the restrooms of the future as fluid, exciting, magical, yet functional spaces, replacing the anodyne and stereotypical toilets of the past. For this designer, who describes himself as an architectural hero, restrooms are places where 'it should be possible to get excited, to dream, to discover ourselves, to find new mates and above all to be creative'.

left
The unisex restroom area is dominated by oversized silhouettes of male and female figures, outlined on the opaque glass doors. The diffuse light bounces off the shiny walls and floor.

opposite
Accents of colour are found in the blue neon words, which announce the washing, drying and soap cells contained in a stainless-steel aperture in the black laminate wall above the sinks.

Four Food Studio
Karim Rashid
New York, USA

Karim Rashid approaches everything he designs in the same way, whether it is a garbage bin, a building or a restaurant. He believes that design touches us on every level and can change the way we perceive the world; and that interiors, in particular, can create very personal human experiences. Karim has coined the expression 'Sensual Minimalism' to describe his style, which has an emotional appeal whilst staying minimal. For him soft, colourful and tactile forms are more human, signifying comfort and pleasure.

The Four Food Studio is certainly warm and calming and was conceived to appeal directly to the senses. The restaurant has four dining and drinking areas, each of which reflects a different season, with the menu changing every 13 weeks to serve only what is fresh and available at that particular time of the year. The four environments have completely different atmospheres, and depending on mood, the clientele can choose between the Spring lounge with lime green upholstery and patterned carpet, the Summer bar where a large projection screen displays abstract graphics of water and nature, the Autumn dining room with warm wooden ceiling and floor and gold glass walls, or the smaller Winter room which, like the interior of an igloo, has only rounded surfaces giving the impression of endless space. Externally, the restaurant is bordered by a glass wall on which rotating images of blossoming flowers, a bright blue sea, falling leaves and a virginal snow field encourage passers-by to enter.

The restrooms were designed as a complete antithesis to the main space. A stark, black and white palette is in high contrast to the front-of-house's rich,

m | 1 | 2 | 3
ft | 5 | 10

left
Floor plan of the Four Food Studio, illustrating the positions of the restrooms, away from the main circulation area of the restaurant, lounge and bar; an intentional device to enhance the private nature of the area.
1 Entrance
2 Cloakroom
3 Reception desk
4 Spring lounge
5 Private dining room
6 Kitchen 7 Summer bar 8 Outdoor dining area 9 Autumn dining room 10 Winter room
11 Female restroom
12 Communal washing area
13 Male restroom
14 Disabled restroom

opposite
View from the Summer bar, through the Autumn dining room, to the exclusive Winter room which has five dining booths and is dominated by a digital fireplace. The cool, igloo-like interior contrasts with the warm woods and gold glass walls of the main eatery.

The communal area, off which the male and female cubicles are located, rises to 4.5 metres (15 feet). Horizontal bands of black, grey and silver glass mosaic emphasize the height of the space. A central glass and mirrored wall divides the atrium and is bordered by individual black glossy glass sinks.

warm and welcoming colours and other surfaces, in particular the gold Curvet glass walls of the Autumn dining room, off which the facilities are located. The main element of the bathroom is the central lobby, which soars to a height of 4.5 metres (15 feet). Symmetrical in design, the male and female bathrooms are split by a glass centre half-wall with mirrors on either side. Cylindrical, glossy black glass sinks, lit from below, are placed on either side. To emphasize the height of the ceiling horizontal monochrome and silver bands of glass mosaic clad the walls. The restrooms are purposefully situated out of the main circulation of the dining rooms and bar to reflect their private function. Although the area is communal, the cubicles (featuring black toilets and black glass shelves and mirrors) are positioned on either side of the wash area, which in turn is segregated by the 2 metre (7 foot) high glass barrier that makes the user feel comfortable in the unisex environment. A tantalizing meeting of hands, however, is allowed through the shared paper towel dispensers that are situated within the mirrored wall.

However, the restrooms have no direct lighting; instead an ambient effect limits unflattering shadows. The fixtures, fittings and surface materials were all selected for their ease of maintenance.

Like the restaurant itself, Karim's design for the bathroom is a seamless experience, one area running into the next to maximize functionality but also to enhance the strong features of the space.

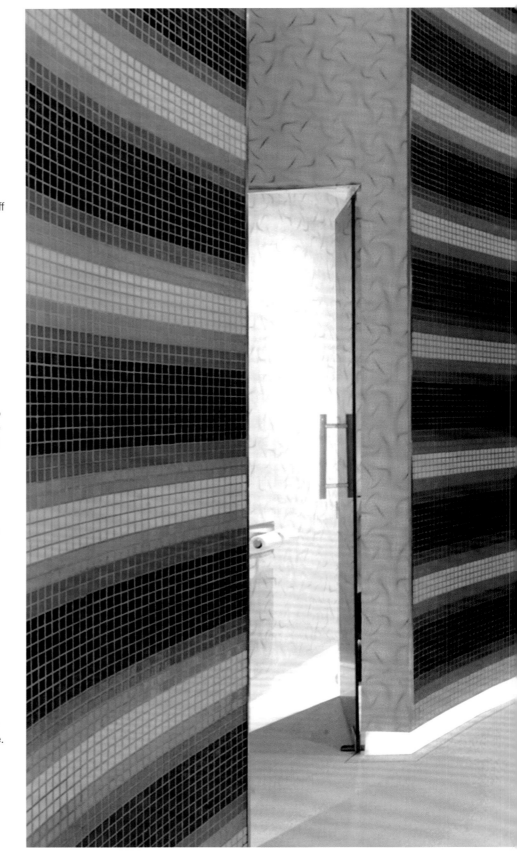

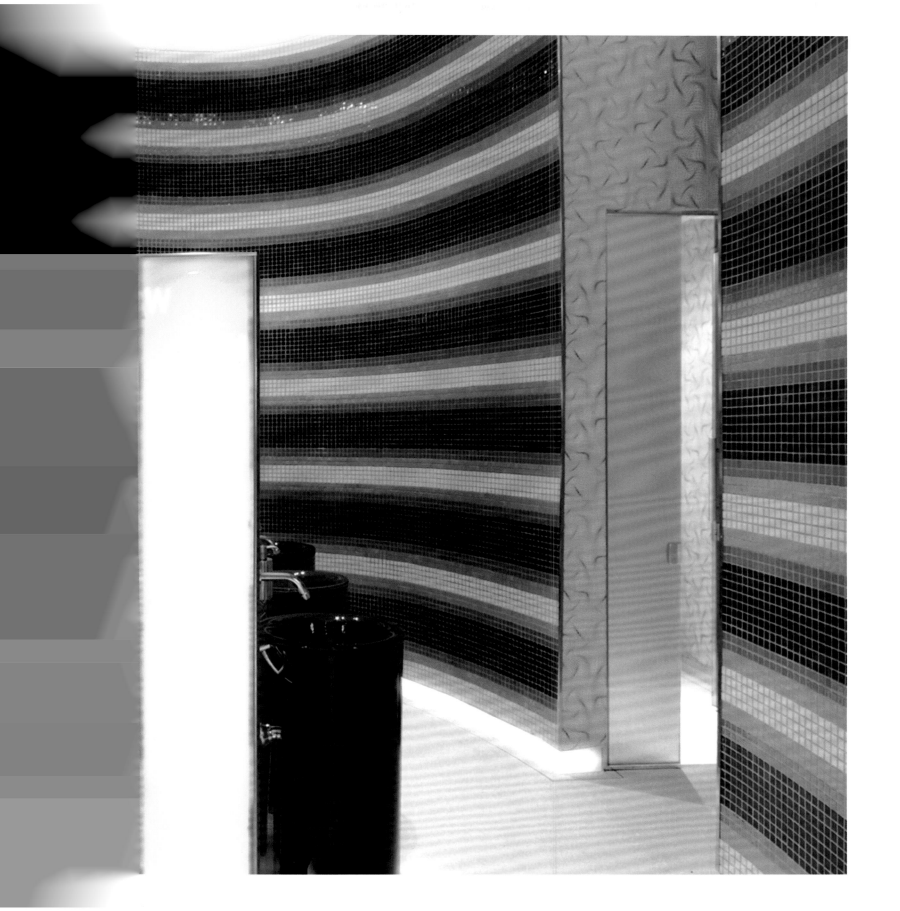

Le Cirque
Tihany Design
New York, USA

right
The interiors have all the fun and exuberance of the circus. They were inspired by the kinetic, abstract hanging wire artworks of Philadelphia-born Alexander Calder (1898–1976). The main dining area sits under a 'big top' custom-made lampshade.

opposite
The corridor to the toilets displays Sirio Maccioni's extensive photo collection of family and celebrities.

Adam D. Tihany's architecture is tailor-made to showcase the unique talents and personalities of his clients. His relationship with the people for whom he works is very intimate and it's only by building up personal portraits that he can adapt his interiors to fit their characters.

Tihany's collaboration with Sirio Maccioni, the owner and creator of Le Cirque, New York's legendary social and culinary landmark, is of many years standing. Together they have built up the restaurant's concept development to reflect Maccioni's exuberant personality, subtly adjusting the design brief from the first incarnation in the early 1980s, through a series of manifestations situated in New York, Las Vegas and Mexico City, to the latest outlet.

As the name would suggest the interiors of all Le Cirque restaurants have in common a heightened sense of the theatrical, with Tihany drawing inspiration from eighteenth-century France, the tumbling acrobats of the Cirque du Soleil and the romantic Italian troubadours, to evoke the fun and excitement of the circus in the various outlets.

The most recent Le Cirque celebrates the Maccioni family's bond with the city of New York. Tihany has fashioned an all-American concept, informed by Alexander Calder's famous kinetic hanging wire constructions, notably his magical circus installations. A 3.5 metre (12 foot) long, suspended wire acrobat mobile hovers above the entrance foyer, the main 120-cover dining area sits below a giant, abstract 'big top' lampshade, while whimsical art pieces add a touch of fantasy and humour to the ambience.

The restrooms continue the theatrical theme. For such a large restaurant they are relatively small, with only four

Restaurants

**First floor plan.
The restrooms are
situated next to the
main entrance and
are relatively small
for the size of the
restaurant, which
contains a main
120-cover dining area
and a 92-seat bar
and café. There is
also a mezzanine for
private functions (not
shown). 1 Restrooms
2 Cloakroom 3 Bar
4 Private dining area
5 Main entrance
6 Main dining area
7 Pastry kitchen
8 Main kitchen with
chef's table**

**The cubicles contain
toilets and washing
facilities. They appear
jewel-like, with the
ambience of a private
dressing room, and
no expense has been
spared on the opulent
materials and fixtures
used. The wire 'bird-
cage' feature light is a
reference to the work
of Alexander Calder.**

cubicles. Each stall contains toilet, sink
and make-up area, forming an intimate
space with the backstage appearance
of a leading lady's dressing room. No
expense has been spared on materials
and fittings, which are in tune with the
quality and luxury found in the rest of the
upmarket interiors. Walls and flooring are
in Honey onyx with black marble inlay,
and Noir St. Laurent polished marble
respectively. Water flows into hovering
stainless-steel basins, suspended over a
solid steel surface. Custom-made, back-
lit oval mirrors are embedded around
their edges with flattering lighting, while
a crystal and wire 'bird-cage' lamp refers
to the work of Calder. A tribute to the
role Maccioni has played in New York's
culinary world, the main feature in the
restroom area is his extensive photograph
collection of the celebrities and politicians
who have visited his restaurants over the
years. Tihany has displayed this montage
on specially designed 'Sirio' wallpaper.

Tihany distinguishes his approach
to design as 'singular and original
thinking with attention paid to every little
detail'. Nowhere is this more evident
then the newest Le Cirque in New York.
Restrooms and restaurant alike combine
materials, fixtures and furnishings to
create the most sensual, surprising and
opulent environments.

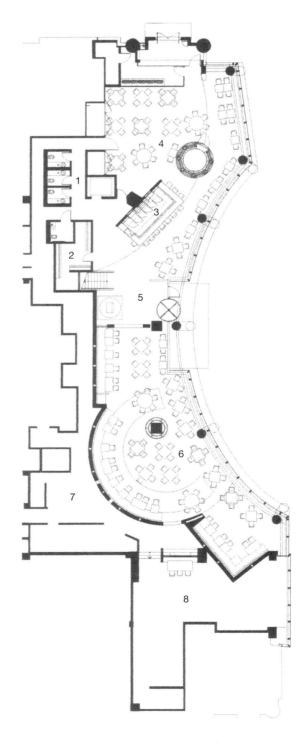

Two and a Half Lemon
Chris Briffa
Birgu, Malta

Two and a Half Lemon bar and restaurant forms part of the restoration programme of the oldest waterfront in Malta and is located in the sixteenth-century limestone vaults that once formed the Treasury of the Knights of Saint John. Chris Briffa's intervention into this listed building had to respect the original fabric of the architecture and any alterations had to be reversible.

Briffa's concept took shape following a visit he made to an art exhibition where he observed how a painting is framed to enhance its impact. Two and a Half Lemon is based on the notion that rather than the 'frame enhancing the framed' the 'framed enhances the function'. All the practical elements of the project – the seating, the low walls and the restrooms – were turned into 'mounts', which contain typical Maltese aesthetic elements.

Drawing his inspiration from the ancient environment of Birgu – vernacular patterned tiles, wrought-iron windows, medieval rooftops and bric-à-brac finds in weekend flea markets – Briffa has combined traditional features with a contemporary aesthetic in a versatile space which can be easily transformed from a bar and restaurant into a private dining room or an intimate cocktail lounge. The decorative patterns on the floor tiles were traced and digitally printed on the upholstered tiles, creating an illusion of hardness on the soft wall. The outdoor seats were decorated with original tiles, outlined in marine plywood. A light wall hiding the kitchen was fragmented with wrought-iron insets. Photographs of the rooftops were printed inside the custom-made shades, and a concrete cube, which contains the toilets, frames a niche of washbasins in front of shelves full of granny nostalgia.

top
The restaurant and bar is situated in sixteenth-century limestone vaults facing the Marina along the oldest waterfront in Malta.

opposite
The project contains very few permanent elements, which means that the interventions are largely reversible. Decorations are based on the traditional architecture and artefacts found in medieval Birgu.

m |1 |2 |3
ft |5 |10

Briffa explains that he had the most fun designing the restrooms and was lucky he was able to convince the client to devote a whole, freestanding concrete room to the male and female stalls and unisex wash area. By creating a space within a space, the architect conceived an area that can be easily changed as wear and tear takes its toll. It also gave the possibility for the restrooms to be used as an exhibition space for local artists. Briffa wanted his design to engage all the senses by using different sights, sounds, textures and ornaments to transform function into art. Two artists, Jon and Sandra Banthorpe, were given the space adjacent to the washbasins to express their notion of locality. The result is a kitsch miscellany of old bits of wallpaper, antique bevelled-glass mirrors and shelves of gloss-white plastic figurines. Sound artists Spookey Monkey were commissioned to compose an experimental soundtrack, but this was replaced by ambient music after a customer complained of hearing 'funny bubbling noises in the bathroom'.

'The restroom is like a raw box full of surprises in a sixteenth-century room, where patrons meet and discuss the absurdities and nostalgia which surrounds them,' concludes Briffa.

left
The sanitaryware is old-fashioned to fit in with the nostalgic ambience of the design. Briffa wanted old cisterns to be placed above the toilet but the client insisted on recessed fittings.

far left
The restroom is located within a raw concrete box which protects the precious spatial qualities of the old room.

opposite left
Floor plan of the restaurant showing the location of the freestanding concrete box containing the toilets to the left of the main dining area.
1 Bar 2 Food bar
3 Kitchen
4 Restrooms
5 Terrace

opposite right
Artists Jon and Sandra Banthorpe created the kitsch decoration of the unisex washbasin area, including antique finds and plastic figurines.

Two Twenty Two
Chris Briffa
Valletta, Malta

top right
Entrance to Two Twenty Two. The concept of the project was to contain all functions of the venue in a single black box, standing detached from the sixteenth-century bastion.

bottom right
The signage on the doors to the male and female restrooms use quotes from the writings of artist Piet Mondrian and architect Mies van der Rohe.

opposite
The female restrooms are aesthetically differentiated from the male facilities by a faceted Murano glass wall and a male mannequin's hand, which is used as a clothes hanger. A green light gives an other-worldly glow to the diurnal atmosphere.

In common with Two and a Half Lemon (see page 136), Chris Briffa was once again commissioned to design an interior for a listed building: this time, an unfinished tunnel, until recently used as a garage space, inside the sixteenth-century bastion wall of Valletta, Malta. However, unlike his earlier project, which featured a decorative refurbishment, Briffa has opted to create a highly stylized restaurant and lounge bar, where high-tech replaces low-tech design and the vernacular has been eschewed in favour of an ultra-modern space.

With restrictions placed on how much the original fabric of the infrastructure could be altered, Briffa has designed what he refers to as a 'mobile kiosk which can be plugged into the ancient fortifications'. Like the freestanding concrete toilet block at Two and a Half Lemon, the intervention in Valletta is a room within a room. The sloping walls of the 'box' – which grows narrower as it recedes into the tunnel – imitate the angle of the bastion that maximizes the space on both ground-floor and first-floor levels while preserving the original volume of the vault. The steel and timber structure is entirely independent of its surroundings and contains its own supply of light, sound, running water and air extraction systems; as such, the bastion walls show no sign of being touched. Dining and lounge areas are separate: the former is adjacent to the self-supporting construction and the latter is on top. Contained within are mechanical systems, storage space, a service hatch and the bathrooms. At the entrance, the 'box' protrudes onto a concrete terrace, which sits in the raw, fortified landscape to form an amphitheatre with views over the harbour.

top and right
The restrooms are housed in a layered plywood structure, which has a rich and sensuous texture. The male restroom uses black bamboo as a dividing screen.

opposite left
**Floor plan showing the restrooms located at the inner end of the structure, adjacent to the kitchens.
1 Outdoor concrete terrace 2 Entry hall 3 Bar 4 Kitchen 5 Downstairs dining area 6 Restrooms**

opposite right
The lines of the wash areas are kept clean by concealing soap dispensers and hand driers behind the mirror. Voyeuristic glimpses into the male and female restrooms are afforded by a window linking the spaces. Ambient lighting glows in soft green.

The restrooms are located at the inner end of the structure. An accommodating client allowed the architect carte blanche to get the maximum impact from a limited space. In line with the concept of the rest of the restaurant, the restrooms are contained in a separate black, layered plywood container which houses all the functions. Lines are kept pure by concealing soap dispensers and hand dryers. Male and female cubicles were conceived as mirror images of each other; their shiny surfaces and mirrored-angled ceiling produce distorted images in the diurnal atmosphere. Although separate, the facilities are linked by a window, which allows voyeuristic glimpses of the occupants in the mirrors above the wash basins. The two areas are virtually identical but subtly delineated by decorative elements: a black bamboo screen in the male facilities and a Murano glass dividing curtain in the female

restroom. Large mannequin hands, male for the ladies and female for the men, are used as clothes hangers and the signage on the doors of the restrooms takes the form of witty quotes from the writings of Piet Mondrian and Mies van der Rohe.

For Briffa restrooms form an important creative element of any project; they are private spaces in which the user can take time away from the busy public areas to allow his or her senses to prevail. The architect's sensuous designs play on this concept and provide surprising encounters, which become focal points within the overall scheme of an interior.

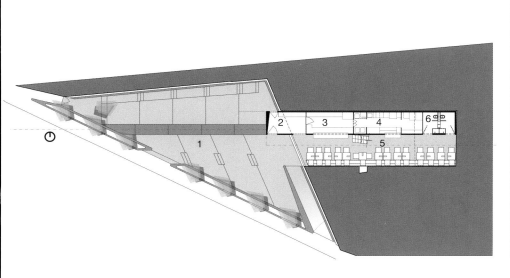

Nobu Fifty Seven
David Rockwell
New York, USA

Although David Rockwell's unique brand of entertainment architecture has been applied to everything from stage sets to airport terminals, he is best known for his theatrical restaurant interiors. The stage has been in Rockwell's blood from an early age. The son of a touring vaudeville actress, he spent his childhood at a community theatre in New Jersey where he and his brothers performed and worked on the sets. At the age of nine, Rockwell's stepfather moved the family to Guadalajara in Mexico; the vibrant colours, people, markets, festivals and bullrings have stayed with Rockwell as vivid memories and informed his colourful, energetic and surprising interior designs.

Nobu Fifty Seven is no exception. The restaurant is the second of Rockwell's collaborations with chef and entrepreneur Nobu Matsuhisa who now has an empire of 15 restaurants dotted around the globe. The original Manhattan Nobu was inspired by *Madame Butterfly* – with stencilled cherry blossoms and chopstick barstools – but for Nobu Fifty Seven Rockwell has adopted a much earthier aesthetic, based on the vernacular of the traditional Japanese fishing villages, with the ocean creating the pervasive theme.

The progression through the interior reads like a stage set. The double-height space is dominated by the staircase, which leads from the first-floor lounge to the second-floor restaurant, allowing diners to make a dramatic 'entrance'. Tables have been sacrificed to this choreographed scene of transition from the hectic world outside to the magic of the Asian aquatic world inside.

The terrazzo floor of the lounge is patterned with ripples, the walnut bar top

floats, like driftwood, atop an illuminated onyx base, while the walls and columns are sheathed in timber-strand shingles as a reference to ethnic Japanese fishing houses. A chandelier made out of thousands of abalone shells links the first floor to the second. In the restaurant above, a giant back-lit banquette of woven albaca, inspired by fishing baskets, undulates like waves throughout the space, while further woven panels stretch across the ceiling, forming a cocoon that is clearly visible from 57th Street.

The male and female restrooms are situated adjacent to the Hibachi table to the rear of the second-floor dining areas and continue the front-of-house design language. Contrasting naturally-occurring materials and textures have been used to create a handcrafted ambience, alluding to marine life and traditional Japanese fishing culture. The walls are either in slate or embedded with black river rocks. The floor extends the slate walls to unify the space, while doors are panelled in rich,

mid-brown American walnut, creating a dialogue between warm and cold.

As in the main dining room, speciality artwork has been used in the restroom for the accessories, most notably the sinks which are hand-carved in granite by Modern Stone Age. Cantilevered from the wall, these give the appearance of having been roughly hewn by Japanese artisans, featuring an irregular surface which contrasts with the smooth finish of the mirrored panels on the wall behind. Lighting is an important element in any interior made by Rockwell, using it as he does to create a mood and clarify a space. In Nobu's restrooms, custom-made sconces, produced from natural fibres laminated in glass, which are back-lit, provide ambient and flattering illumination, while down-lighters highlight the toilets and urinals. The fittings were chosen for their simple, minimalist lines and the spotlights provide vivid accents in an otherwise muted and relaxing space devoted to human ritual.

left
The inspiration for Nobu Fifty Seven is Japanese fishing villages, with the ocean providing the pervasive theme. The bar area is dominated by a giant chandelier made from thousands of abalone shells, linking the double-height space with the restaurant above.

opposite
The main feature of the restrooms are their custom-made carved granite sinks which cantilever out from the walls. Contrasting naturally-occurring materials and textures, black river rocks, slate and American walnut have been used to create a handcrafted ambience.

Posto
Studio UdA
Turin, Italy

Posto is a four-storey renovation located in a corner section of an historical building in central Turin. The project includes a kitchen in the basement, cafeteria and takeaway on the ground floor, a sales and display area for CDs and magazines on the mezzanine, and a sit-down restaurant on the fourth floor. The concept was to develop a design which could easily extend into a chain of fast-food restaurants and in which 'sense perception' is key to the aesthetic: sight and touch are stimulated by a variety of materials which have been used to delineate the formal arrangement of space.

The client Stefano Cecchi is a partner in the George V Restauration group, which has opened renowned venues around the world, such as Barfly, Barrio Latino, and the world-famous Buddha Bar in Paris. His experience in hospitality and retail, as well as his knowledge of the recording industry (he owns his own studio) inspired his multi-media concept for the fast-food chain. His brief to Studio UdA, a practice well known for its experimentation with technology and constructive techniques, was to create a space that could be easily transposed to other locations and be effortlessly legible in its demarcation of functions: eat-in, take-out, food preparation areas or retail.

In collaboration with Cucco studios in Milan, which specializes in the expressive and purposeful uses of advanced materials, UdA's architecture becomes a microcosm in which images, screens

left
The entrance to the restaurant restrooms announces the ethereal space that lies beyond.

oppposite left
The restrooms on the fourth floor are for the use of the sit-down restaurant. They are reached along a corridor lined with glowing multi-layered glass partitions, embedded with orange Vanceva film.

opposite right
Visitors to Posto have their sense of reality suspended through shadows and reflections.

and reflections work together to take the customer out of his or her normal comfort zone. The interiors balance opaque and colourful screens with clear surfaces, iridescent with warm lighting effects and graphics of video art in a multi-sensory experience. Enlarged, back-lit landscape photographs and a chill-out soundtrack complete the effect.

There are two sets of restrooms in the restaurant. On the ground floor, the first is a utilitarian affair with disabled facilities. All fixtures, fittings and finishes on walls and floors were chosen for easy maintenance.

However, the unisex, orange glass restroom cubicles on the fourth floor, adjacent to the sit-down restaurant, continue the ethereal theme of the rest of the restaurant. To obtain a monolithic effect, a custom-made steel structure has been used to suspend the multi-layered glass panels with a semi-transparent film insert. Black Corian boxes fixed to the walls contain photoelectric cells which provide washing facilities and air-drying automatically. Neither water nor any hint of the accessories usually found in a restroom can be seen, which subverts the users' sense of normality.

The restrooms become a place of meditation and play on notions of perception by highlighting shadows, reflections and mirror images. The resultant sensation is alienating. Acting in miniature for the rest of Posto, UdA's design mixes reality with imagination in a space that suspends belief.

left
The restrooms on the ground floor, which include disabled facilities, have been finished in steel and opaque glass, chosen for their ease of maintenance. The utilitarian atmosphere alludes to the fast-food element of the business, a cafeteria and a takeaway, which are also located on this floor.

far left
In the restaurant restroom on the fourth floor, Corian boxes are used instead of sinks. Equipped with photoelectric cells, they provide soap, water and air-drying automatically. They eliminate the accessories usually associated with washrooms, which has the effect of subverting the users' sense of reality.

opposite
To create a monolithic effect, the doors to the restaurant toilet cubicles have been hung from a custom-made steel frame.

The Commune and The Press Room
Leigh & Orange
Beijing and Hong Kong, China

The Commune is one of the two restaurants to be found in The Clubhouse, a multi-villa complex which sits in the shadow of the Badaling section of the Great Wall. Part boutique hotel, part rural retreat and part showcase of contemporary architecture, the commission invited Asia's most avant-garde designers to create modernist buildings at angles in the lush forest, an hour's drive from Beijing. The Clubhouse, designed by Seung H-Sang, is the central hub and, as well as the restaurants, contains a private theatre, a library, bars and an art gallery. Leigh & Orange were brought in to design the 80-cover Chinese restaurant, which retains the elegant yet severe architectural style of the original structure, while bringing an element of fun and a club-like aesthetic to the interior.

At the other end of the scale, The Press Room is a modern European brasserie located on the fashionable Hollywood Road in downtown Hong Kong. The restaurant is so called because the building in which it is situated was once home to one of the city's best-known newspapers. To pay homage to this heritage, Leigh & Orange's brief was to create a space which featured the patina of age combined with a dynamic 'hot-off-the-press' atmosphere.

Both restaurants have distinctive, contrasting styles but are linked in their use of an unusual range of materials and furnishings to create an eclectic aesthetic that continues in the restrooms. Hugh Zimmern, project architect for both venues, believes that while creativity should not get in the way of functionality, the design of bathrooms is of utmost importance, highlighting the needs of the clientele to be entertained and surprised.

top left
General shot of the interior of The Commune. Seung H-Sang's minimal use of concrete, Cor-ten steel and wood has been leavened by an exotic and rich palette of locally sourced materials.

bottom left
The female restrooms are finished in dark wood veneer and black leather.

opposite top
The male and female restrooms at The Commune switch sexual stereotypes. The male facilities are finished in shades of pink with delicate crystal chandeliers.

opposite bottom
The main feature in both male and female restrooms is the continuous form of the hand-beaten copper sinks, shown here in the male facilities.

bottom left
The Press Room creates a relaxed ambience by using distressed leather for the banquettes, an easily chipped paintwork on the walls, as well as Jean Royère and Art Deco influenced light fittings and furniture.

bottom right
The main feature in The Press Room restrooms are the cubicle doors, which are finished in plastic laminate with a *toile de jouy* motif which mixes French eighteenth-century imagery with scenes of 1950s Hong Kong.

opposite
The male restrooms have a retro 1950s ambience, with large floor-mounted urinals, shiny white wall tiles and lights.

The Commune's restrooms switch sexual stereotypes. The male area is outlandishly feminine in shocking pink with crystal chandeliers, simply constructed from glass pieces strung on fishing line and hung beneath standard MR16 recessed down-lighters. The female restroom is the exact reverse and is finished in dark wood veneer and black leather with ambient lighting coming from decorative pieces made out of chemistry tubes, flasks and Liebig condensers. The client wanted more than just toilets, so the rooms double as a smoking area for the men and a powder room for the women. Restricted to locally sourced materials, the architects were forced to 'think outside the box', and the main feature in both rooms is the custom-made continuous form of the hand-beaten copper sinks.

The Press Room takes the hybrid European/Chinese restaurants prevalent in Hong Kong during the 1950s and

1960s as inspiration for its restrooms. They have large floor-mounted urinals, white wall tiles and quarry tiles on the floors. The decorative lights, painted in a red oxide colour, are influenced by the French mid-twentieth-century designer Jean Royère, while the vanity top is made from Chinese 'Mountain/Water' marble used extensively in antique Chinese furniture. The overriding feature, however, are the cubicle doors, which have been finished in plastic laminate with a *toile de jouy* motif. The eighteenth-century fabrics produced by the Jouy factory traditionally depicted scenes of pastoral idyll, set in magnificent settings. In The Press Room, the pattern has been customized to include images of 1950s Hong Kong.

East meets West in the restrooms of The Commune and The Press Room. Both illustrate what can be achieved on a limited budget by using inexpensive yet unusual materials, creating interest through pattern and strong tonal contrast.

Embryo
SquareOne
Bucharest, Romania

right
Shot of the basement restaurant with its elliptical 'skylight' into the bar above.

opposite top
Male and female restrooms use similar textures and colouring; Marin refers to them as 'yin/yang complementaries'. The restrooms complement the unusual, fluid and imaginative interiors of the nightclub.

opposite bottom
Basement (left) and ground floor (right) plans showing the location of the restroom areas. The circular walls of these spaces were created by studying movement fluxus within the toilets.
1 Restaurant
2 Bar 3 Cloakroom
4 Basement restrooms 5 Circular bar 6 Lounge
7 Entrance 8 Ground floor restrooms

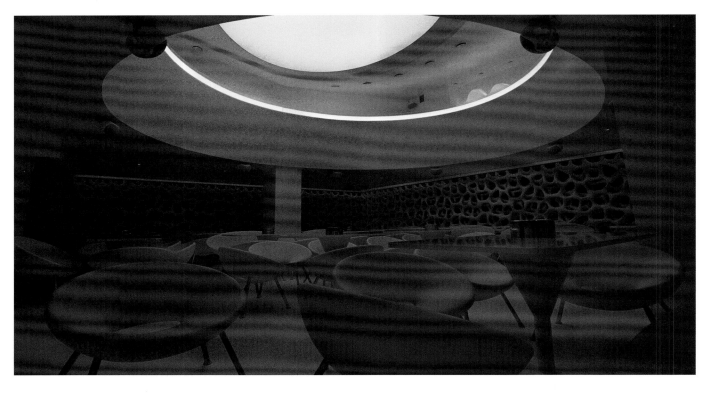

The design of Embryo takes its inspiration from pre-life or life on a cellular level. The building it occupies is unremarkable, the only hint of what lies behind the façade is a bright red band of Exalcobond with Syplex inserts, depicting a graphic line of embryos in various stages of development, reaching maturation on the glass doors of the entrance. Moving along the horizontal cone which forms the foyer of this two-level nightclub, however, is like making your way into a Barbarella fantasy land; a futuristic, pop environment of glossy, organic forms. In the basement, the restaurant is in white epoxy suffused with constantly changing light. The wardrobe is red-walled and pierced with circular holes through which the coats are collected. The ceiling which has an elliptical opening, becomes part of the floor of the glowing white bar above. Mounting a set of stairs, again in epoxy, the lounge has a crimson wall cut through with bands of white light punctuated with fittings comparable to nuclei. The seating is designed by Philippe Starck and the tables are custom made by SquareOne and come replete with built-in ice buckets.

It's the kind of nightspot that pervades the West and is derivative of the works of designers such as Karim Rashid and 3deluxe. However, this is Romania and it has to be remembered that this is a country which is only slowly emerging

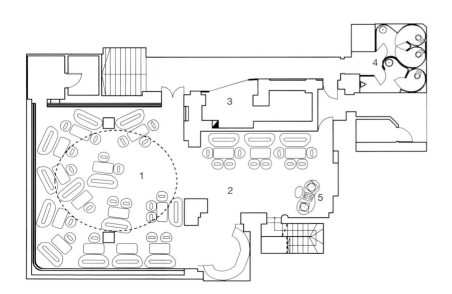

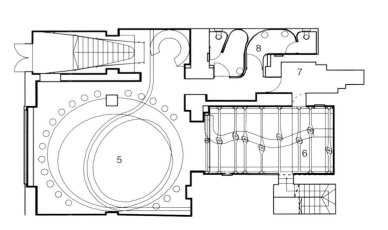

from the restraints of communist architecture. Richard Marin, co-founder of SquareOne, writes: 'In my opinion, the contemporary Romanian architectural stage is divided into 85 per cent almost-unbearable architecture, 13 per cent "correct" architecture and a final 2 per cent that is done in a way that takes an interest in how it affects the life of its inhabitants and how it is a part of this place and moment in time.' Thanks to a brave client who gave the architects carte blanche to do whatever they wanted, Embryo's playful and exotic aesthetic shows evidence that Romania is beginning to find its design edge.

The restrooms at Embryo are a microcosm of the overall concept; they are unusual and fluid and leave room for imagination. The design of the toilets (there is one in the basement and one opposite the ground-floor entrance) arose from the restricted spaces the architects were given. Marin and his partner Adrian Cancer made diagrams of movement through the area to determine the minimum square area needed to get all the functions in place. The result informed the curved nature of the walls which define the most essential dynamic flux. The waved aspect was enhanced by the horizontal pattern of the mosaic and by ensuring the sanitary fittings were as freestanding as possible.

Marin compares the design of a toilet as being 'as important as a cool ringtone on a mobile phone, as long as it does its simple task of alerting its owner it can bear any message and become a tool of social interactivity'.

left
The horizontal bars of the 'Trend' mosaic emphasize the wavy nature of the walls. Sanitaryware is kept as freestanding as possible to add to the sense of flow and movement.

Embryo

Chinawhite VIP area and Volstead
Satmoko Ball
London, UK

If you want to go and star-gaze, then there are no better places to do so than Chinawhite and Volstead, which attract A-listers on a nightly basis. That is if you can get in.

Situated around the corner from one another close to Piccadilly Circus (which under the watchful gaze of Alfred Gilbert's *Eros*, has been the vibrant centre of London's club land since the 1950s), both venues conceal themselves behind minimal doorways. You wouldn't know they were there unless you were a member of the in-crowd; and that's the point. With all-night opening, and a red-rope policy, these highly stylized and themed nightclubs are the epitome of exclusivity, with no expense spared on their seductive interiors.

Chinawhite first opened for business in 1998. However, a refurbishment of

bottom
The interior of the VIP Mao Room at Chinawhite carries on the oriental theme of the rest of the nightclub.

opposite
The unisex restroom is approached under the intense gaze of an Andy Warhol–inspired portrait of Chairman Mao and is usually manned by an attendant who supervises flow through a red rope into the restricted space.

left
The cubicles in
Chinawhite are tiny
and contain classic
ceramic toilet pans
with wooden seats.
Brass detailing adds
a reflective surface to
make the small space
appear larger.

right
Mirrors, lights
and candles have
been skilfully used
to enhance the
space. Materials
were selected for
their warmth and
tactility as well as
their durability. The
ceiling is lined with a
luxurious silk canopy
and the sinks are
made from veined
slate and timber, and
are filled with pebbles
through which the
water drains away.

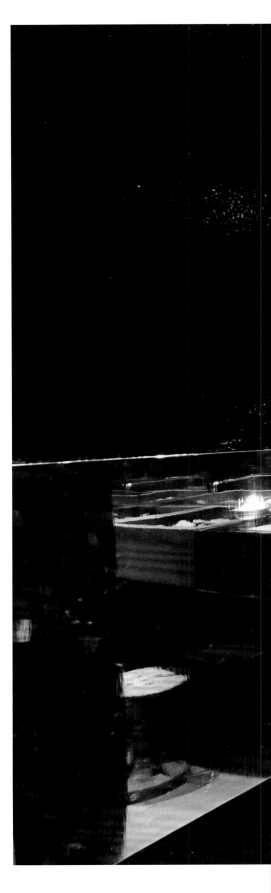

top right
Volstead's interiors are inspired by the concept of the speakeasy and use dark polished surfaces, lush leathers and fabrics, fine veneers and Art Deco detailing to create a luxurious, subterranean environment.

bottom right
The Volstead toilets were designed as glossy black boxes. The tiling and joinery were kept simple and the sanitaryware is classic, serving to highlight the lights and detailing.

opposite
The machine-age taps, fun pull flushes, stainless-steel plinths and Art Deco lights were selected to complement the speakeasy aesthetic of the nightclub.

the VIP area, including ensuite unisex restrooms and a bar area, was carried out since. The new interior, the Mao Room, continues the original oriental theme. Like Bedouins, guests lounge on exotic daybeds strewn with rich tapestries and opulent cushions, under parasols of raw silk and amid exotic artefacts, their every move monitored by a rather disquieting Andy Warhol-inspired portrait of Chairman Mao. Sitting below him, a male attendant dressed as one of Mao's followers mans the toilets, allowing only male or female guests to enter at any one time.

Cara Satmoko and Adrian Ball have carried on the aesthetic of the club into the restroom, which includes two cubicles and two basins in a tiny 6.5 square metre (70 square foot) space. Careful consideration has been given to materials, equipment and lighting to make the most of the tiny area. A space-enhancing mirror on one wall reflects the stalls opposite and is surrounded by diffuse lights and candles, which add to the overall sumptuous effect. A richly patterned red silk ceiling is the only overt link to the rest of the club's Asian and exotic feel and is set against simple gloss-painted surfaces and brass detailing. Forming an attractive feature, the beautifully veined slate and timber basins are filled with pebbles through which the water drains away. All materials were chosen for their durability as well as their tactile sense of luxury.

Volstead is a subterranean bijou private-members club named after the author of the eponymous Act (Minnesota senator Andrew Volstead) which heralded prohibition in America. The speakeasy interiors were conceived as an ironic take on the flapper era of the 1920s. Chinawhite's owners recommended their favoured architects, Satmoko Ball, to design the interiors. Taking as their base the architecture of Viennese modernist Adolf Loos, they worked with references to the era: wood panelling, Art Deco detailing, veneers and rich leathers and fabrics, combining these influences with allusions to punk (notably the graphics inspired by the Sex Pistols on the settees) and a disco-like Mirroflex ceiling and adjacent mural. 'We have tried to mix iconic style, luxury and wit, using dark polished surfaces, lush materials and beautiful light to make up a rich,

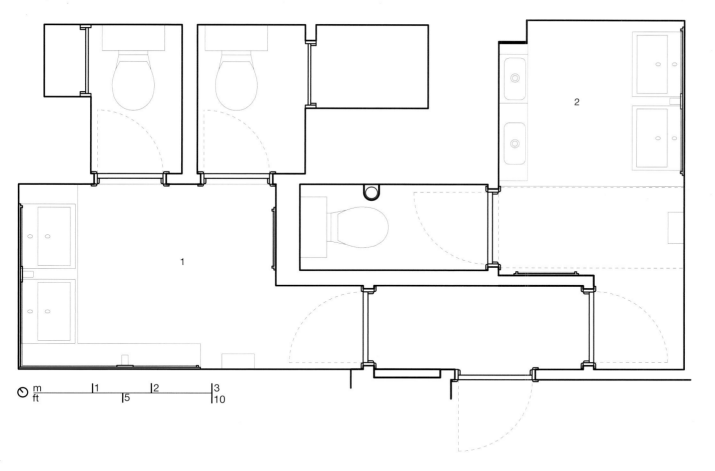

left
Floor plan of the restroom areas in Volstead. The spaces were designed to be space efficient due to the restricted site. The male and female rooms have the same design, although the female restroom has a slightly increased floor space to allow for extra mirrors and an area in which to make up. 1 Female restroom 2 Male restroom

opposite
The shiny surfaces and chrome accents catch the light and visually increase the 18 square metre (194 square foot) space.

intoxicating, surreal take on clubbing in the city,' says Adrian Ball.

In common with Chinawhite, the restrooms occupy a small area, in this case 18 square metres (194 square feet). Servicing the whole of the nightclub, the male and female units were designed to be space efficient, with materials and fittings in tune with the aesthetic of the club. The basement location meant that the ceiling height was restricted due to the existing structure and new ventilation ductwork. Mirrors were used to visually increase the space. The dark tiling, granite flooring and gloss-black cubicles were kept simple to enhance the wall lights and sanitaryware. Classic, almost traditional designs were selected for the WCs, basins and urinals, which were set against machine-age winged airship taps, decorative pull flushes and stainless-steel basin plinths. Chrome has been used to accent the space, catch light and add sparkle to the chiaroscuro atmosphere.

The restrooms in both Chinawhite and Volstead illustrate what can be

made of a limited space. While toilets are obviously not as important as the front-of-house, Satmoko Ball recognize that they should become talking points that the clientele look forward to experiencing. The locations have completely different aesthetics and yet share an emphasis on the tactility of the materials used, which compensates for their diminutive sizes. Perception of quality often comes from what a place feels like to touch. On limited budgets the architects have created intimate yet luxurious environments for these regularly frequented rooms.

CocoonClub
3deluxe
Frankfurt, Germany

bottom left
The techno club is based on the human cell. A membrane wall, composed of perforated concrete panels, allows an osmotic exchange of guests. 'Cocoons' form pods where guests lounge and watch the dance floor.

bottom right
The reception booth for the lavatory attendants is made from plywood covered in white formica.

opposite
The design of the restrooms was conceived as a counterpoint to the opulence of the club and restaurant interiors. The anthracite grey colour scheme gives the space a monolithic and archaic ambience. All technical equipment and functional fittings take a discreet backseat.

The interdisciplinary design firm 3deluxe have gained international recognition for their computer-generated organically shaped forms, their strong graphics and their experimental interior designs. Their architecture mixes the real with the virtual and is based partly on multi-media technology and partly on the built environment. Interiors explore the use of new techniques, atmospheric cyber-lighting and flexible materials in spaces which are futuristic, other-worldly and bionic.

The Cocoon nightlife complex comprises a techno club, two destination restaurants and lounging areas. In common with many of 3deluxe's projects the concept has a biological derivation. The club is based on the metabolism of a cell with the various activities – eating, drinking, lounging and dancing – being allocated different areas analogous to the organelles of a cell. The main dance floor is the interior of the organism with the DJ and VJ pulpit cantilevered above,

forming the nucleus. The whole area is surrounded by a membrane wall, which people can pass through in both directions; a constant osmotic exchange of guests.

The Micro Club Restaurant and Bed Restaurant Silk offer the chance to break from the hectic activities of the nightclub; the former has a diurnal aesthetic and acts as an adjunct to the club, while the latter elevates eating and drinking to the level of an artistic ritual based on ancient eating ceremonies.

The restrooms act as a counterpoint to the opulence of the club and restaurant interiors. There is an almost archaic overtone to the design, emphasized by the use of an anthracite grey colour scheme and the texture of the randomly arranged ceramic wall tiles. White side lights enhance the textures. A seamless black terrazzo floor forms a stark colour contrast to the light grey, plastered ceiling. The ceramic sinks are installed in a row on a masonry plinth in front of a wall-to-wall mirror illuminated from above by a single strip, emitting diffuse

light. LCD monitors above every sink are concealed behind the two-way mirror and project images which appear to be superimposed on the glass. Pinkish-violet toilet partitions stand out by way of their colour and design. The surfaces are adorned with graphics conceived by 3deluxe which seem to change depending on how far away the observer stands. Composed of pine branches mirrored several times, from a distance the pattern appears to be abstract in the form of a Rorschach inkblot, while viewed from up close it resolves itself into the Asian-style motif found in other areas of the club. The cubicle doors close automatically after use, preventing any prolonged break in their embellishment. Loudspeakers set into the suspended ceiling allow music from the nightclub

to penetrate the restrooms. The overall architectural design comprises an ingenious spatial arrangement, which made it possible to forgo doors to close off the male and female areas, allowing uninterrupted movements between corridor, lobby and toilet zone.

Even though the design of the restrooms is based on 'less is more', in common with the rest of the club, stylistic elements create a positive stimulation of the senses. 'We do not design the space itself but the experience of the people spending time there,' comment 3deluxe.

top
The ceramic wash basins are set on a concrete plinth. At every sink there is a video image projected by the 15 centimetre (6 inch) LCD monitors concealed behind the two-way mirror. The technical trick creates a fascinating projection effect as the image appears to be directly superimposed onto the mirror glass.

opposite
The cubicle doors are embellished by graphics which take the form of a Rorschach inkblot. The doors close automatically.

Crobar
ICRAVE Design
New York, USA

The interior design practice **ICRAVE** is synonymous with high-octane, energy-driven spaces, which actively engage visitors in their environment. Crobar, situated in fashionable Chelsea, Manhattan, exemplifies its design philosophy and heralds a return to the superclub of the 1980s. Along with the world famous Avalon nightclub designed by the Desgrippes Gobé Group, Crobar was instrumental in introducing a new form of clubbing to New York which, under the iron fist of former Mayor Rudolph Giuliani, had gone through several years of indifference, with nightspots opening and closing virtually overnight.

The club is housed in a former industrial warehouse-type building and occupies an entire city block. The concept was to create a 'fantasy nightclub playground for adults, and the backdrop for a multitude of events, from headline DJs to fashion shows and corporate events'. The design has three distinct spaces (the Main Room, the Reed Room and the Prop Room, which is for the use of VIP guests) choreographed to incorporate different programmes for different users and provide a fresh experience in each environment. The Main Room is the vibrant epicentre of the venue and can accommodate 1,500 clubbers. The dance floor is surrounded by sculptural arches which support a wrap-around mezzanine, a video-projection wall, DJ booth and 'LED ticker' which floods the area below in ever-changing lighting effects. The Main Room is connected to the Reed Room by way of an alienating 'white noise' tunnel, which invites a moment of pause before entering the 250-capacity bar. The Reed Room bears the architectural heritage of the original

right
The PVC tubes in the male restroom were purchased through a construction company and form an inexpensive screen between the main area and the restrooms.

opposite
The restroom can be viewed from the corridor through the PVC tube wall. Some of the apertures are mirrored to allow a degree of privacy.

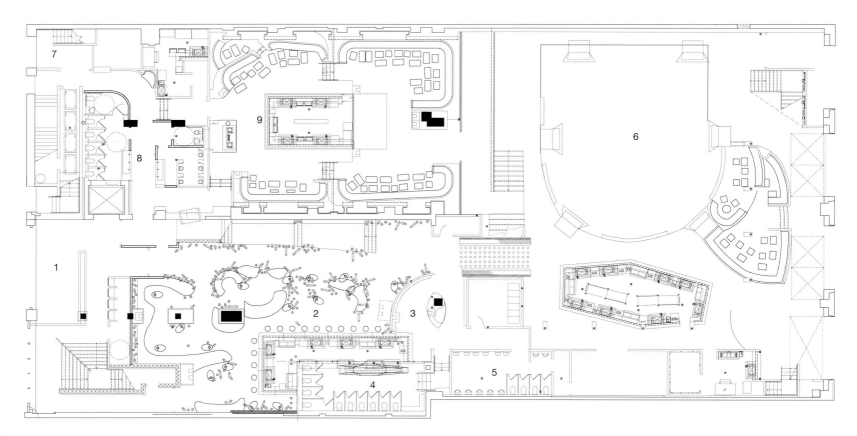

building with open-grate ceiling and exposed brick work but is dominated by contemporary, towering yellow resin 'reeds' illuminated from within. The VIP area is a subdued and intimate loft-like space which retains the original wooden beams of the warehouse. The barrel-shaped ceiling has been lined with burnished copper leaf to add a luxurious element to the industrial aesthetic.

The male and female restrooms were conceived to act as 'hinges' where the experiences of the three environments overlap. They were both designed on a limited budget. In the male toilets, cut PVC tubes, purchased through a construction material supply company, were an inexpensive way to provide a screen between the Main Room and the toilets. Although some of the tubes were left open, others were filled by either mirrors or 'funky' Japanese graphics to add a degree of privacy to the peek-a-boo concept. The urinal wall features repeated Andy Warhol-inspired silkscreens of a bikini-clad woman, which ICRAVE used as a reference to the 1980s club scene. The figures, which are protected under a layer of glass, can

be seen from the corridor through the tubular PVC screen, adding a decorative element to the public space. The female restrooms are situated on a platform overlooking the bar to the Reed Room. In common with the male facilities, they have a flirtatious approach, with a cascading coil metal curtain acting as a 'wall' through which women powdering their noses can both view and be viewed. Both bathrooms are entered through a communal lounge situated between the Main Room and the Reed Room.

'We wanted the bathrooms to be playful and sexy, and part of the whole club experience, not separate from it,' conclude the designers.

left
The female restrooms are situated on a platform overlooking the bar of the Reed Room. A cascading metal chain curtain acts as a wall and allows peek-a-boo glimpses into the space below.

bottom
The wall in the mens' room behind the urinals is decorated with silkscreen prints of a bikini-clad female body inspired by the works of Andy Warhol, which ICRAVE used as a reference to the nightclubs of the 1980s which influenced the design of Crobar.

opposite
Floor plan showing the position of the male and female restrooms situated off the Main Room and Reed Room respectively. A communal lounge links both facilities. 1 **Main entry** 2 **Reed room** 3 **Restroom lounge** 4 **Female restroom** 5 **Male restroom** 6 **Main room** 7 **VIP entry** 8 **VIP restroom (not illustrated)** 9 **VIP lounge**

Reina Bruja
Tomás Alía
Madrid, Spain

top right
The dance floor is dominated by the Metacrilato columns, which are reflected in a mirrored back wall, making them appear to stretch to infinity. The side walls are in faceted mirror, which produces mind-altering effects. Computer controlled LEDs flood the area with up to 16 million colour combinations.

bottom right and opposite
In comparison to the club's organic and highly designed interiors, the restrooms have an angular, almost clinical aesthetic, with exposed plumbing, stainless-steel sinks and classic ceramic pans adding to the industrial ambience.

The male and female restrooms at the Reina Bruja nightclub are tucked away in a discreet corner at the back of the site. Apart from urinals and a smaller floor plan for the male restrooms, there is no difference in their design. The key to the club and its restrooms is light; an ever-changing kaleidoscopic extravaganza which is constantly changing the atmosphere and the appearance of the interiors of the entire venue.

Tomás Alía is one of Spain's leading trend forecasters. His spaces mix the ethnic and the traditional; using avant-garde materials and with an emphasis habitually on the lighting, his designs are young and cosmopolitan.

In the interiors of the Reina Bruja, he has combined light, colour and curved surfaces to make the space morph as the evening progresses. The LED technology is such that 16 million colour combinations create a club which can be used for a variety of activities, from

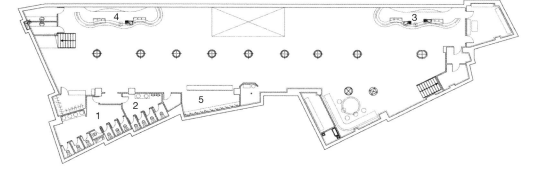

dancing and chilling to hosting private or corporate events. In this last case, the computerized LED system can be adapted at ease to the organizer's expectations, decorating the club, for example, according to the corporate colour scheme of the company or the favourite colours of the host.

The club is situated in Madrid's trendy Callao district and has a futuristic aesthetic which appeals to its trendy clientele. The light emphasizes the organic design in which curved lines are of particular significance. Alía has designed the furniture and fittings with the lighting effects in mind, adopting different geometric shapes from the hall, where the triangle-shaped retro bar welcomes the clientele, to the white counters made of Corian, which soak up the colours. Nine cylindrical columns in Metacrilato have been placed down the centre of the dance floor and dominate the space. Each has floral decorations changing hue. Faceted mirrored walls to the side, and an infinity mirror to the rear, double the space to create mind-altering reflections.

Alía considered the restrooms as extra rooms in the overall scheme; as 'intimate extensions where guests could mingle and bond in a more intimate environment'. The long and narrow site of the club made it difficult to find a location for the bathrooms, a restriction which also dictated a straightforward design of cubicles along one wall, facing the washbasins opposite. The fixtures and fittings were kept simple. Classic ceramic Keops toilet pans were selected to make the most of the coloured LED lights. Stainless-steel sinks and urinals display their plumbing, giving the space an industrial aesthetic, while surfaces are highly glossed to maximize the light. Within the concept of the club's highly styled and sensuous interiors, Alía has opted for a rather clinical non-design in the toilet areas. The most important element is, of course, the lighting. As within the rest of Reina Bruja, colours create varied sensory experiences as they continuously change the appearance of these otherwise unremarkable spaces.

top right and bottom
**As with the rest of
the interiors, colours
constantly change
the appearance
and atmosphere
within the otherwise
unremarkable spaces.**

bottom left
**A geometric light
installation draws the
visitor to the rear of
the club and to the
restrooms.**

opposite
**Floor plan showing
the restrooms tucked
away at the rear of
the site. Nine columns
divide the dance floor.
The chill-out zone is
to the front of the club
and two undulating
Corian bars serve the
clientele. 1 Female
restrooms 2 Male
restrooms 3 Bar 1
4 Bar 2 5 Cloakroom**

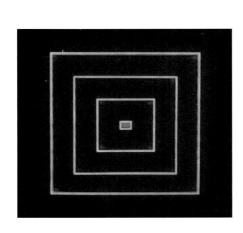

Eve
David Hicks
Melbourne, Australia

The Eve club is a vibrant venue in downtown Melbourne with a nightly clientele of approximately 700, a large majority of them women. It is located in a basement and as such has no direct contact with the world outside. Taking this as his inspiration, interior designer David Hicks created an environment which could adapt to the imagination of its patrons. He wanted a different look for Australia and decided on a retro aesthetic that would bring to mind discos of the 1970s and early 1980s when going out for a night on the tiles was a glamorous thing to do.

A staircase from the entrance leads down into the main space. As there are no allusions to life outside the four walls the hermetic dance floor could be anywhere: on a 1970s cruise ship, in New York's Studio 54 or in a glamorous hotel in Las Vegas. The design has the effect of transporting its patrons into different time periods, cities and environments.

The location of the restrooms was dictated by the fact that the waste points had already been placed in the concrete slab prior to building work commencing. This turned out to be serendipitous as it meant the toilets had to be located near to the entrance of the club, making them easily accessible from the main dance floor and also the VIP area by way of a second side door.

The client's brief was for a unique space which could also integrate into the

right
**The restroom
interiors are cave-
like shimmering
spaces finished in
black glass and shiny
mosaic tiles, which
create jewel-like
environments.**

opposite top
**The lounge has
a retro aesthetic
and is finished in
opulent materials and
baroque furnishings.**

opposite bottom
**View towards the
lounge. The club
is situated in a
basement and as
such has no direct
visual contact
with the street,
which inspired the
architect to create
an environment
that adapts to the
imagination of
the clientele. The
dance floor could
be on 1970s cruise
ship space, in New
York's Studio 54 or
a glamorous hotel in
Las Vegas.**

overall concept for the interiors. The male and female facilities are announced by double-entendre graphics: a black snake and pussy cat. The zones are almost identical, although the ladies' are larger to accommodate a continuous make-up bench. Hicks conceived cave-like environments of shimmering black glass. Shiny mosaic tiles are used uniformly on floor, walls, benches and ceiling, creating a jewel-box effect and allowing an easy focal transition from the dark bar area. Splashes of red are introduced as a subtle reference to the famous Elizabeth Arden red door, an influence that links to the cerise theme found in the rest of the club. Lighting is important to the design as it complements the reflective nature of the surfaces. Intense light focuses on mirrors and washbasins (glass rose-shaped wall lights for the ladies and low-level spot lights for the men) while other areas are allowed to recede into shadow, giving the space a theatrical yet intimate ambience. The overall effect is subdued, in keeping with the light levels in the rest of the interiors. Concealed speakers allow the music from the club to pervade the area. The ladies' room has a full-length make-up mirror running down one wall.

When conceiving restrooms for entertainment spaces Hicks always looks at the opportunity to be creative. Experiences have to be heightened and the area given impact. Although functionality in choice of materials, easy maintenance and low consumption toilet flushes were taken into account, the restrooms at Eve offered a chance to advertise the club's overall design concept and they have become a talking point, drawing new visitors to the venue.

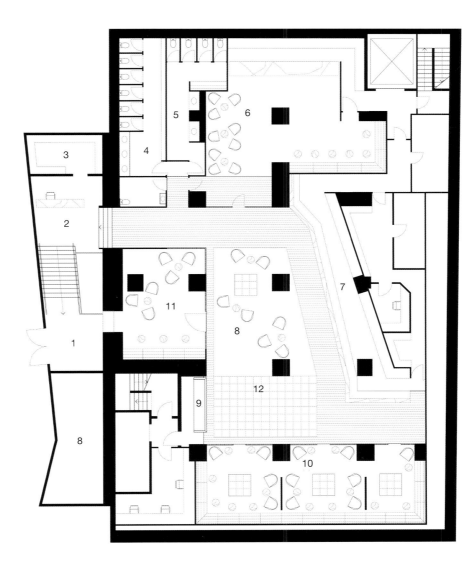

left
Floor plan showing the restrooms situated near the stairs, which descend from the ground-floor entrance, making them easily accessible from the main dance area.
1 Entrance
2 Reception
3 Cloakroom
4 Female restrooms
5 Male restrooms
6 Dragon bar 7 Main bar 8 Courtyard 9 DJ booth 10 Tiger room 11 Garden room 12 Dance floor

opposite
The entrances to the cubicles are in red, which alludes to the famous Eizabeth Arden red door found throughout all her spas worldwide.

185

Eve

Sol & Sombra
Tomás Alía
Madrid, Spain

Tomás Alía's maxim is to 'bring aesthetics to the greatest possible number of people'. Known for his nightlife interiors which harmoniously combine ethnic objects with the most contemporary of materials and lighting effects, his latest creation, the Sol & Sombra lounge, is situated in the traditional Las Letras quarter of Madrid, the neighbourhood with the greatest bull-fighting tradition of the capital.

The design for the nightclub, which offers live concerts of ambient music, including what Alía calls 'flamenco-chill', is a departure from his more avant-garde interiors such as the Reina Bruja (see page 178) whilst still adopting many of their vanguard elements. Alía takes his inspiration from the streets, and from the cultural mix of big cities. The Sol & Sombra is a perfect synthesis of the essence of the *corrida de toros* and a young and cosmopolitan demand for

the modern and innovative. The merit of the project resides in the way he has combined the essence of the bullfight with an original style; reinventing aspects of bullfighting aesthetics – Spanish hairpins called *peinetas*, tooled leather, men on horseback – as elements of modernity.

The façade is clad in dark wood, reminiscent of the old taverns of Madrid, and acts as a contrast to the bright open environment inside, which is swathed in

bottom
The restrooms are located at the end of the narrow site, away from the main circulation points of the club. The wash area in both male and female facilities is dominated by a full-wall mosaic in front of which the modern, streamlined basins contrast with the antique consoles on which they sit.

opposite
Entrances to the cubicles are via back-lit screens decorated with iconic silhouettes of the Iberian bull.

an ever-changing colour mix thanks to a state-of-the-art LED-based light system. The interiors mix ethnic materials such as wood and leather with contemporary elements: fibreglass, futuristic bottle shelves and a wall punctuated with cubic lighting elements.

The blend of old and new continues in the restrooms, which are situated at the end of the long and narrow site, away from the main circulation points of the club. Apart from urinals, the male and female areas are indistinguishable, with basins standing on antique consoles in front of baroque mosaics. Backlit screens of metacrilate etched with iconic Spanish bull silhouettes separate the cubicles from

the washing area. The fixtures and fittings are modern and streamlined to contrast with the furnishings, which Alía says 'look as if they have been rescued from the period between the wars'. As with the rest of Sol & Sombra the restrooms' ambience is constantly changed by LEDS, which alter the hues within the toilet cubicles.

Tomás Alía's interiors are always fun and this is nowhere more apparent than in Sol & Sombra, which breathes new life into the Spanish clichés of bullfighting and flamenco. Alía likes to work on restrooms, recognizing them as an area where his clientele mix, bond and 'enjoy themselves'. Not wanting the bathrooms

at Sol & Sombra to stand in isolation from the rest of the interior, he refers to the concept behind his design as a futuristic bullfight poster; a magical environment in which the users lose themselves in a world of Iberian luxury and make-believe.

Project credits

WC1 (2006)
Architect/Designer The Marchhare
www.WC1.co.uk
Project team WC1, The Marchhare designers, Indigo Blue project management and build
Client WC1

Hasuikebori (2005)
Designer Akira Watanabe & Masahiro Ikeda
Client Imperial Household Agency, Department of Works

Aire de Merle and Grans and Saint-Martin-de-Crau motorway (1995)
Architect Beguin & Macchini
www.beguin-macchini.fr
Civil engineer/steel structure Caltec
Quantity surveyor Eric Loiseau
Civil engineer for concrete/plumbing Cert Angers
Main contractors BEC (for Grans and Saint Martin), Gardiol (for Aire du Merle)
Manufacturers Ferrari (pre-stressed fabric at Air du Merle), Villeroy and Boch (tiles), Bega (lighting), Presto (taps), Duravit (toilets and urinals)
Client A.S.F. (Autoroutes du Sud de la France)

Urilift and UriGienic (2002)
Designer Marco Schimmel
Manufacturer Urilift International BV
www.urilift.com

Multi-storey car park (2006)
Architecture Comprehensive Design Architects
www.allerdale.gov.uk/toilets-art
Interior surface design Paul Scott and Robert Drake

City-Toilet 2=1 (2005)
Designer Wall AG in cooperation with GK Sekkei
www.wall.de

POINTWC (2006)
Designer Nina Virus, Studio5491
www.studio5491.com
www.pointwc.com
Manufacturers of washbasins, urinals, toilets Roca, Laufen
Client Eric Salles/LETS

Osaka Castle Park (2005)
Architect/Designer Shuhei Endo Architect Institute
www.paramodern.com
Project team Shuhei Endo Architect Institute
Client Osaka City Hall Department of Housing General Office

Museum of Applied Arts Café (2006)
Architect/Designer Eichinger oder Knechtl
www.eok.at
Client Betriebsgesellschaft österreicher im mak

'Belle et Fou' Theatre (2006)
Architect Meuser Architekten BDA
www.meuser-architekten.de
www.belle-et-fou.de
Project team Natascha Meuser, Miriam Lammel
Toilets, urinals Laufen
Flush Grohe DAL
Brushes Dornbracht
Washbasins, taps Toscoquattro
Towel dispenser Agape
Waste paper baskets, tissue holder, lotion dispenser Keuco
Client Spielbank Entertainment GmbH

Crèche (2004)
Architect RCR Aranda Pigem Vilalta Arquitectes
www.rcrarquitectes.es

Artoteek refurbishment (2005)
Architect NEXT Architects
www.nextarchitects.com
Project team Marijn Schenk with Ica van Tongeren
Tile design Ica van Tongeren
Client Michiel Morel, Artoteek

De Effenaar backstage restrooms (2005)
Designer Bob Copray & Anthony Kleinepier
www.bobcopray.nl
www.anthonykleinepier.nl
Main contractor interior Retera interiorworks
Client Effenaar

Office of the Children's Commissioner (2006)
Architect/Designer Feilden + Mawson
www.feildenandmawson.com
Main contractor BW Interiors
Flooring Armstrong
Lighting Modular Lighting Instruments
Taps, washbasins Duravit
Toilets Ideal Standard
Client The Office of the Children's Commissioner

Maag Recycling Factory (2006)
Architect Oos
www.oos.com
Project team Christoph Kellenberger, Andreas Derrer, Severin Boser, Lukas Bosshard, Benedict Ramser, Ana Lucia Widmer-Peniagua
Client Maag Recycling, Max Maag AG

Dr Finkelstein's Orthopaedic Practice (2005)
Architect Mateja Mikulandra-Mackat
www.mikulandra.de
Lighting concept Mateja Mikulandra-Mackat
Lighting construction firm eTs
Construction supervisor Jörn Grünert
Tiles Bisazza
Top wash-basin Alape
Toilet bowl Duravit
Fitting for wash-basin, paper roll rail, toilet brush Dornbracht
Soap dispenser Keuco
Client/Owner Dr. Matthias Finkelstein

Dental Clinic KU64 (2005)
Architect/Designer GRAFT (Lars Krückeberg, Wolfram Putz, Thomas Willemeit)
www.graftlab.com
Project architect Tobias Hein, Karsten Sell
Architects Sven Fuchs, Lennart Wiechell
Project team Björn Rolle, Markus Müller

CCA Graduate Center prefabricated restrooms (2004)
Architect Jensen & Macy Architects
www.jensen-macy.com

Geberit Headquarters (2005)
Designer/Architect Jérôme Gessaga & Christof Hindermann, designrichtung gmbh
www.designrichtung.ch
Graphic design Simon Burkhardt
Client Geberit AG

Hotel Puerta América (2006)
www.hotelpuertamerica.com
Design John Pawson, Ron Arad, Zaha Hadid, Sir Norman Foster, Plasma

Blue Heaven Radisson SAS Hotel (2005)
Architect/Designer Tihany Design
www.tihanydesign.com
Project team Adam D. Tihany (Principal),

Carolyn Ament (Senior Designer), Peter K. Lu (Interior Designer), Andréa Riecken (Senior Designer and Project Manager), Francesca Caputo (Designer)
Operator Radisson SAS Hotels & Resorts
Executive chef Oliver Schakow
Architect of record John Seifert Architects
Kitchen consultant K3 planungsbüro
Lighting designer Isometrix Lighting + Design
Structural engineer Schüßler-Pla
MEP engineer Ingenieurbüro Walter Maier
Acoustical consultant ITA Ing.ges.f techn Akustik mbH
General contractor Reuter Innenausbau GmbH & Co. KG
Millwork Reuter Innenausbau GmbH & Co. KG
Glasswork Reuter Innenausbau GmbH & Co. KG
Decorative lighting MoreLight
Brasserie decorative lighting Zonca SpA
Restaurant rose chandeliers Moss
Carpets Motta Moquettes
Custom furniture Colber srl (bar and dining chairs, bar stools), Rupert App GmbH+Co (wine display and stair), Otto Valenta (restaurant metal buffet)
Sink Axolo s.r.l.
Stalls partition Schaefer Trennwandsysteme GmbH
Fittings Stangls
Client Radisson SAS Hotels & Resorts

Sofitel (2005)
Designer Perron
www.perron.com
Photography Sheena Haywood
Client Sofitel Queenstown

Hotel Duomo (2006)
Architect Ron Arad Associates
www.ronarad.com
Project team Ron Arad, Julian Gilhespie, Geoff Crowther, James Foster, Asa Bruno & Taishi Kanemura
Executive architects Pierandrei Associati
Lighting consultant David Atkinson Lighting design (DALD)
M & E engineers Andrea Raggini, Studio Elettoprogetti
Structural engineer Milco Fregnan
Client Pierpaolo Bernardi

Lloyd Hotel (2003)
Architect/Designer MVRDV in collaboration with Christian Seyforth and Atelier van Lieshout
www.lloydhotel.com
www.mvrdv.nl
www.ateliervanlieshout.com

Club Privé at the Ballagio Hotel (2005)
Architect/Designer Tihany Design
www.tihanydesign.com
Project team Adam D. Tihany (Principal), Nikola Gradinski (Project Manager and Designer), Mavette Maton (Designer), Peter K. Lu (Interior Designer)
Operator NYLC LLC

188

Architect of record HLW
Lighting designer Ann Kale
Structural engineer Lochsa
MEP engineer & Kurtz
General contractor Penta Group
Millwork Quality Cabinet
Decorative lighting Baldinger Architectural Lighting
Stone Coverings etc.
Carpet Sacco Carpet
Custom furniture Vaughn Benz
Brand for faucets Vola
Brand for toilets Toto
Client Bellagio

Ono at the Gansevort Hotel (2004)
Architect/Designer Jeffrey Beers
www.jeffreybeers.com

Mix at THEhotel (2004)
www.thehotelatmandalaybay.com
Interior design Patrick Jouin
www.patrickjouin.com
Interior design project team Patrick Jouin & Director Sanjit Manku with Marie Deroudilhe (Project Architect) and Claudia Del Bubba (Senior Interior Designer)
Architecture firm Klai Juba Architects
Project architect Robert White
Owner Mandalay Development
Sound design Savi
Custom millwork Mueller Custom Cabinetry
Lighting L'Observatoire International
MEP engineering JBA Consulting Engineers
Structural engineering Lochsa Engeneering
Graphics Philippe David
General contractor Mandalay Development
Client rep 1027 Design Management

Bon Moscow (2006)
Design Philippe Starck
www.philippe-starck.com

Nobu Berkeley ST (2005)
Design David Collins Studio
www.davidcollins.com
Client Como Holdings

Morimoto (2006)
Architecture Tadao Ando Architects and Associates
Design team Tadao Ando, Masataka Yano, Stephanie Goto Design Group, Stephanie Goto, Principal, Ross Lovegrove Furniture Design
Main contractor Certified of NY
Project manager Gardiner and Theobald
PR firm Full Picture (lifestyle) / Baltz and Co. (food)
Lighting consultant Isometrix
Graphic designer Patricia Spencer
M&E engineer Thomas Polise Consulting Engineers
Structural engineer Leslie E Robertson and Associates
Bottle wall consultant FRONT
Ceiling feature contractor Showmotion Inc.

Facade fabricator Zahner
Special feature consultant Takeshi Miyakawa
Concrete consultant Reginald Hough
Geotechnical engineer Langan
Furniture Poltrona Frau
Owner Starr Restaurant Organization, Stephen Starr
Manufacturers Showmotion, Inc (ceiling), Bam Bam Designs (bathroom partitions), Electrix (bottle wall feature), Takeshi Miyakawa (bottle wall bar), Kohler (sinks in bathrooms), Duravit and Toto Neorest (toilets), Vola (faucets)
Cabinetwork and custom woodwork Erik Cabinets

'P' Food and Wine (2006)
Architect Simone Micheli
www.simonemicheli.com
Client Region of Piedmont

Four Food Studio (2005)
Architect/Designer Karim Rashid
www.karimrashid.com
www.fourfoodstudio.com
Project team Karim Rashid, Camila Tariki, Dennis Askins
Main contractor Rosner Construction
Flooring manufacturer Plyboo Wood Floor, Durite Terrazzo, Durkan Custom Carpet, Vidrepur Glass Mosaics
Other manufacturers Dornbracht (tap), Vitraform (washbasin), Porcher (urinal and toilet), Black Glass by Curvet (stall)
Client 515 Restaurant Group

Le Cirque (2006)
Architect/Designer Tihany Design
www.tihanydesign.com
Project team Adam D. Tihany (Principal), Rachel Cunha (Project Manager), Amrei Schmidt-Fumian (Senior Designer), Mavette Maton (Designer), Peter K. Lu (Interior Designer)
Operator NYLC LLC
Executive chef Pierre Schaedelin
Architect of record Costas Kondylis & Partners
Kitchen consultant Cini-Little International, Inc
Lighting designer Focus Lighting, Inc
Structural engineer WSP Cantor Seinuk Group Inc.
MEP engineer Jaros Baum & Bolles Consulting Engineers
Acoustical consultant Cerami & Associates Inc.
General contractor Structure Tone, Inc.
Millwork Peterson Geller Spurge, Inc.
Glasswork A-Val Architectural Metal Corp.
Decorative lighting Baldinger Architectural Lighting
Stone and tile Interior Design Flooring Corporation
Carpet Sacco Carpet
Wire sculpture Tim Flynn
Custom wallpaper DesignTex , BMG Imaging
Custom Furniture Colber srl
Graphic designer Mirko Ilic Corp. (New York, NY)

Client Sirio Maccioni, Le Cirque Owners
Rep Jim Finnerty Consulting, Inc

Two and a Half Lemon (2006)
Architect/Designer Chris Briffa Architects
www.chrisbriffa.com
Project team Chris Briffa, Jennifer Barth, Simon Brugaletta (Architects), Jon and Sandra Batnthorpe (Installation Artists)
Contractor and consultants Stanley Falzon, Alan Debattista
Client Davide Cachia

Two Twenty Two (2006)
Architect/Designer Chris Briffa Architects
www.chrisbriffa.com
Project team Chris Briffa, Jennifer Barth, Darren Cortis, Laurence Briffa, Bernard Vella
Contractor and consultants Attard Bros. (civil works), SAW ltd. (carpentry), J Lautier (glass & steel)
Client Desmond Vella

Nobu Fifty Seven (2005)
Architect/Designer David Rockwell
www.rockwellgroup.com
Main contractor Shawmut Design
Flooring in the restrooms Stone Source

Posto (2003)
Architect/Designer UdA
www.uda.it
Project team Andrea Marcante, Massimiliano Comoletto, Valter Camagna
Co-workers Guya Chatrian, Luca Talarico
Structural project Ing. Treves
Electrical system project Ditta Alfa Engineering
Furnishings F.lli Groppo
Iron items Ditta Pedro
Glass items Cristal King
Electrical system Ditta Tarditi
Plumbing/air conditioning system B & M. Impianti
Construction company Impresa Recanzonc

The Commune (2003)
Architect Leigh & Orange Ltd
www.leighorange.com
Project team Hugh Zimmern, Ricky Hung
Main contractor Dibang Interior Architect Const Ltd
Consultants PBA, Pacific Lighting Ltd.
Copper basins manufacturer LAEC Construction Ltd
Client Soho China Ltd.

The Press Room (2006)
Architect Leigh & Orange Ltd
www.leighorange.com
Project team Hugh Zimmern, Teresa Tang, Alice Leung
Main contractor Ocean Contracting Ltd.
Consultants Sunland AL (Int'l) Co. Ltd., Pacific Lighting (HK) Ltd
Decorative lights manufacturer Ricardo Lighting Ltd.
Plastic laminate manufacturer Formica
Urinal + basin manufacturer Tangshan

Huida Ceramic Co Ltd.
Client AAP Investment Ltd.

Embryo (2006)
Designer Square One
www.squareone.ro

Chinawhite VIP area (2006)
Architect/Designer Satmoko Ball Ltd.
www.chinawhite.com
Main contractor Rhema Building Services Ltd.
Manufacturer of flooring Burlington Slate
Taps Sheardown
Washbasin William Garvey
Client Chinawhite

Volstead (2006)
Architect/Designer Satmoko Ball Ltd.
www.volstead.com
Main contractor Dales Contract Ltd
Manufacturers of flooring Rocco Stone, Victorian Woodworks
Wall tiles Reed Harris
Lighting Davey Lighting, Tobias Grau
Taps, wash basin, toilets Lefroy Brookes
Urinals Twyford Slab Urinal
Accessories Samuel Heath
Client Ignite Group

CocoonClub (2004)
Architect/Designer 3deluxe
www.3deluxe.de
Tiles Mosa
Floor Rockies
Faucets Hansa
Towel dispenser, waste paper bin Wagner Ewar
Washbasins, urinals Keramag

Crobar (2003)
Designer ICRAVE in collaboration with Bigtime Design
www.icravedesign.com
Project team Lionel Ohayon, Siobhan Barry, Tonya Rife, Shawn Hope (ICRAVE), Callin Fortis (Bigtime Design)
Faucet Sloan
Sink Whitehaus
Urinal Toto
Contractor Bond & Walsh
Lighting designer Focus Lighting
Client Crobar Worldwide

Reina Bruja (2006)
Designer/Architect Tomás Alía
www.tomasalia.com

Eve (2006)
Designer/Architect David Hicks
www.davidhicks.com.au
Manufacturers Bisazza Tiles (flooring), Megalit, Axolight (lighting), Architectural Hardware (taps), Caroma , Britex (washbasin, urinals, toilet), Britex (accessories)
Client Dorsia

Sol & Sombra (2006)
Designer/Architect Tomás Alía
www.tomasalia.com

Index

Picture credits

The publisher would like to thank the following sources for permission to reproduce images in this book:

Tomás Alía (178–81, 186–7); Amiaga Photography (130–1); Patricia Bailer (112–15); Paul Beaudoin (59, 61); © Bettmann/CORBIS (7 bottom middle); BFI (11 top middle right); Tom Bisig, Basel (42–3, 78–81); John Chapple/Contributor © Getty Images (9 middle left); Stephen Chernin/Stringer © Getty Images (9 top right); Copyright the Artist; courtesy Sadie Coles HQ, London (11 bottom middle left); © Mat Collishaw (11 top left); Thomas Duval (109); Stephen Elvidge (9 top left); © Alberto Ferrero (82–3, 96–7, 148–51); Fox/Photofest (9 middle right); redrawn by Gregory Gibbon (7 bottom left); Gladstone Pottery Museum, Stoke-on-Trent (7 middle left); © Martin Godwin 2006 (9 bottom right); Caroline Greville-Morris/Redferns Music Picture Library (11 bottom right); Hiepler Brunier Architekturfotografie (74–5); © Allard van der Hoek (98–100); © Werner Huthmacher (48–51, 70–1, 73 left); Nicu Ilfoveanu (158–61); Jensen & Macy Architects (76–7); © J.R. Krauza (175, 177); Eric Laignel (108); Roger Lee (28–31); Michiel van Lierop (58, 60); © Atelier van Lieshout (101); © Fredrika Lökholm & Martin Slivka (62–5, 104–7, 110–11, 120–3, 132–5, 144–7, 156–7, 162–5, 166 bottom, 167–8); Maurizio Marcato (124, 126–7); Andrea Martiradonna (88–91, 102–3); Mary Evans Picture Library (7 top, middle and bottom right); Yoshiharu Matsumura (12–13, 38–41); Trevor Mein (182–4); © Christian Michel (24); © Christian Michel/VIEW (22, 25); M. Mikulandra-M (72, 73); NEXT architects/Ica van Tongeren (56–7); John Nye (152–5); © Frank Oudeman (174); © Anne-Françoise Pelissier (34–7); Perron (92–3); © 2005. The Philadelphia Museum of Art/Art Resource/Scala, Florence and © Succession Marcel Duchamp/ADAGP, Paris and DACS, London 2007 (11 top right); David Pisani (136–43); Polygram/Photofest (11 bottom middle right); © Eugeni Pons (52–5); Emanuel Raab for 3deluxe (170–3); S.M.A.H. (125); © Shinkenchiku-sha (18–21); Kolin Smith (129); © Rupert Steiner (44–7); Simon Tegala (94–5); Troika Photos (9 bottom left); Universal/Photofest (11 bottom left); Simon Upton (116–19); Urilift International BV (26–7); © Vanni Archive/CORBIS (7 top left); © Rafael Vargas (84–7); Wall AG (32–3); WC1 (14–17); © Dominique Marc Wehrli (www.wehrlimueller.ch) (66–8); © Mark Whitfield (166 top).

Author's acknowledgements

I would like to thank the architects and designers featured in *Restroom* for all the time they have taken in helping me to write this book, the photographers for their wonderful pictures, and my friends and family for putting up with my countless anecdotes on the subject of toilets!!!

At Laurence King I owe a great dept to my editor, Zoe Antoniou for her help and advice, Kim Sinclair for her skill in the production of the book, and Laura Willis for her marketing and publicity expertise.

To those working outside of the company, my thanks go to Nicola Homer for her copy-editing and Kim Richardson for the proofreading of the manuscript. Above all I would like to acknowledge John Round for making the book look lovely and for never once complaining and to Fredrika Lökholm for her patience and dedication in researching the book with me. I would also like to show my appreciation for the remarkable images which Fredrika and Martin Slivka shot whilst on location in London and New York.

I'm flushed with gratitude to you all.